A Doubter's Guide to the Bible

A Doubter's GUIDE TO THE Bible

Terry Giles

Abingdon Press
Nashville

A DOUBTER'S GUIDE TO THE BIBLE

This book is printed on acid-free paper.

Library of Congress Cataloging-in-Publication Data

Giles, Terry.
A doubter's guide to the Bible / Terry Giles.
p. cm.
Includes bibliographical references (p.).
ISBN 978-0-687-65833-6 (binding: pbk., adhesive perfect : alk. paper) 1. Bible—Criticism, interpretation, etc. 2. Bible—Miscellanea. I. Title.
BS511.3.G55 2009
220.6—dc22

2009011778

09 10 11 12 13 14 15 16 17 18—10 9 8 7 6 5 4 3 2 1
MANUFACTURED IN THE UNITED STATES OF AMERICA

For my family

CONTENTS

INTRODUCTION

WHAT'S WRONG (OR RIGHT) WITH DOUBT?

This book sucks!" So was fired the opening salvo from a first-year university student in response to my question, "Why would anybody read the Bible, let alone take a university course on it?" It was the first day of what proved to be a lively and enjoyable semester.

I teach at a fine university. One of the unusual things about this school is that every student is required to take an introductory course on the Bible. I suppose you've guessed it—I teach that course. At the beginning of the semester it has become my habit to ask each class questions designed to give me some sense of the students' predispositions toward the Bible. While not stating it quite as succinctly or forcefully as the student I quoted above, many, many share her opinion. Although it sometimes takes a while for the group to uncover and fully understand the rationale for their feelings, they usually have some pretty good reasons for their viewpoint.

But before I tell you about the rest of the conversation, let me pause a moment. I'm telling you about this opening day of class because the students I work with are very much like the rest of us, but with one exception. The people in that classroom are not shy about expressing what many of us feel. So, although you may not be ready to conclude that the Bible sucks, perhaps you can identify with a degree of uneasiness about the Bible—a certain doubt that nags at you. If so, you may find it interesting how this opening day conversation generally evolves.

DOUBT HAPPENS

After the first couple of bold responses, things begin to get exciting. It's fun to stand back and watch the mental wheels turn as these people talk with one another about why they feel the way they do. At first, when it becomes evident that the vast majority of people in the class (usually between eighty and one hundred) have doubts about the Bible, the room is filled with an awkward discomfort. People aren't sure what to think about all this. Some, especially the first-year students, get fidgety, wondering if somehow or other they crossed a line and voiced an opinion or asked a question they weren't supposed to ask. But after a few minutes of reassurance, and after the group figures out it's OK to say what they really think, the floodgates open and a lively discussion ensues. Without exception, the discussion has always evolved to voice some important questions about the Bible that, frankly, should make all of us think twice about paying attention to it or to those who claim to speak for it. For some, the questions and doubt stem from the scandal of discredited religious figures and organizations. For others, doubt about the Bible comes from the many and contradictory claims made about the Bible and from the hopelessness they feel about ever finding meaningful answers in the Bible. Over the last five or six years one of the greatest objections and reasons for doubt about the Bible has been the growing perception that religion in general and the Bible in particular are so enmeshed in violence and conflict that, truth be told, we would all be better off without them.

Yet, the conversation never stops at this point. Despite the recognition of some serious difficulties encompassing the Bible right now, these students are not content with leaving it there. The most amazing part about their conversation is that, again without exception, the conversation always includes the recognition that despite all the problems, the Bible is somehow important and must be dealt with. Even those who have never opened a Bible (and the number is quite large) sense that, particularly in America, the Bible has played an important role. It's just that the serious doubts these people have about the Bible are calling into question the usefulness of the Bible in the world they will be forming in the coming years.

THE COURAGE TO DOUBT

Since the title of this book attracted your attention, and since you've made it this far into the introduction, I assume you too have doubts about the Bible. Doubt is inevitable for people, who, for whatever reason, are compelled to ask, *why?* In and of itself, doubt is neither right nor wrong, neither good nor bad. It simply happens when past confidences are called into question. But, as I've discovered, and as you may already know, doubt isn't easy, and usually there is a price to be paid for asking the hard questions. All too often doubters raise questions that others find uncomfortable. Doubt can isolate the doubter. The discomfort that others feel by the doubter's questions is frequently translated into anger or guilt directed toward the doubter. That anger and guilt is most painful when it comes from unexpected sources: friends, family, or religious compatriots. I've felt it, and I suspect you have too. If so, please understand that you are not alone and there will be no anger or guilt found here. In these pages, a fair-minded pursuit of answers to nagging questions is encouraged. In these pages, you may not find all your doubts resolved or all your questions answered. Some of the answers offered here may not satisfy you. This book makes no pretense to being the final word. My hope is that we will journey together for a while, sharing our questions and discovering new answers.

ONE LAST THING

Before we leave this introduction, permit me one last thing. The Bible is a book, to no small degree, about God. Even though God is not the subject of this doubter's guide, writing any book like this one on the Bible that does not mention God is like trying to ignore the eight-hundred-pound gorilla in the room (I hope God won't mind the analogy!). So I feel it only fair to tip my hand a bit. Some of what you will read in this book comes through the filter of my own experiences, both good and bad. Authenticity demands it. Yet, having said this, I do not assume your experience with God (should you even admit to a God) will have been the same as mine. In fact, your experience may be quite different. So I will not attempt to impose my experience onto you and I trust you will not allow it either. You need not approach this book from a particular religious vantage point in order to engage the questions we ask. My hope is that together we can put our doubt to good cause. I will try to bring you into a conversation regarding some of the most important issues concerning the Bible that are facing us today. In so doing, I will try to provide perspectives and viewpoints that have been beneficial to me. I don't pretend to have all the answers to the questions we will consider, and I certainly don't expect that you will always agree with those answers that have worked for me. I am convinced, however, that if the Bible is to have a continued presence in the twenty-first century, it will be because people like you and me have asked our hard questions and have put the Bible to the test. So, for now, I'm glad for your company. Let's see where our questions will lead.

CHAPTER ONE

DOES THE BIBLE REALLY MATTER ANYMORE?

Why should anybody bother with the Bible? It's a fair question and where we must begin. After all, the world has changed pretty drastically since the Bible's pages were written. Not many of us keep wandering flocks of sheep, live in a small dynastic kingdom, or sacrifice cows in the backyard (unless the summer backyard cookout gets out of control!). But there's more. Not only is there a great gulf between the way we live and the way people in the Bible lived, but also how we think about the world around us has changed tremendously from how people in the Bible thought about their world. So if the Bible does matter, if it is going to have a continued place, the first condition that we need to consider is the very fact of change.

A FLY IN THE AMBER

I recently watched a fascinating television show that illustrated the matter well. The show was a science special featuring researchers intent on the examination of insect life from long, long ago. Apparently, at a time in the far distant past, some poor little bugs had become stuck in gobs of pine pitch that have, over the millennia, solidified into amber stone, with the little critters still entombed and well preserved inside. These little insects are frozen in time, preserved in pieces of transparent amber stone and visible to curious onlookers from the outside.

For many, this is what the Bible has become. It is an ancient collection of strange and old writings available to the curious onlooker. Stuck and lifeless, just like those little insects, the Bible is frozen in time. In many instances, those entrusted with its teaching and preaching have led us here. They arrive at this point from two quite opposite directions.

Some, especially among those of us in colleges, universities, and other academic settings, follow a path that is focused largely on the past. Content to explore all that can be known about the circumstances of the Bible's composition and compilation, we find it easy to avoid asking why and how this particular collection of documents has had such tremendous power and influence. It's much safer to content ourselves with the dispassionate examination of an inanimate relic from the past, peering into its pages much like the biologist gazing into the amber stone. I don't mean to say this kind of inquiry is unimportant—for indeed it *is* important! The age of the biblical books, where they came from, and the condition of their preservation are all valuable pieces of knowledge. These are important things to know if we are going to make sense of the Bible. But these sorts of things don't tell the whole story. Stopping here leaves the Bible a curiosity from the past, frozen in amber stone.

Others have chosen a different path. Reacting against the tendency to treat the Bible as frozen and lifeless, a thing of the past, some, particularly in the religious trades, argue for the Bible's vibrancy and eternal relevancy but also end up with a fly in the amber. They are persuaded that the Bible is changeless, unmoved by its changing circumstances and environment, just like those poor little bugs. Convinced that the Bible is anything but dead and lifeless, they attempt to simply read its words within the context of our own place and time, forgetting that the writers of the Bible were citizens of a world quite different from our own. In a sense, those on this path assume the way we see it now is the way it's always been. They appeal to the timeless relevancy of the Bible without providing evidence to back the claim. It's almost as if the Bible simply dropped out of the sky, never touched by the realities of time, culture, and history. The Bible becomes a parenthesis in time, thought to be equally applicable anytime, anyplace. Part of the wonder of the biblical books is that they do speak to fundamental human issues shared by us all, and so in a sense the message of the Bible is timeless. But the ways those issues are addressed in the pages of the Bible always bear the marks of the time and place in which they were written.

Unfortunately, when applied without consideration to culture and environment, the Bible becomes a perversion of its former self. A religious *Jurassic Park* is created in which the span of time between the Bible's writing and our day is collapsed, with the assumption that the Bible will communicate now just as it did when first written. But when removed from the time and culture of its origin and simply dropped into a foreign environment, the Bible can become just as misplaced and potentially dangerous as the dinosaurs of the movies.

Regardless of either path taken—viewing the Bible as only an artifact from the past, or effectively denying that the Bible has a past—the result is the same. The Bible, itself, as it was written and as it influenced the world in which it was written, becomes like those little insects, nothing more than a fly caught in amber.

CHANGELESSNESS AS A SURE WAY TO AVOID DOUBT

A sure way to avoid doubt about the Bible is to keep it securely closeted in the past or proclaimed timeless and independent from the processes of history. Safely removed and unchanging, the Bible becomes free from doubt but totally irrelevant. It is reduced to nothing more than a curiosity from another time and another place or it is forced to assume a voice imposed on it by those who seek to bring it into the world of today.

But let's face it—times have changed. The world we live in is far different from the world of the Bible. The fundamental differences between these two worlds naturally lead to some doubts about the Bible today. Let's explore some of the changes that have occurred.

CHANGE IN THE DEFINITION OF TRUTH

The first change that we need to consider is a fundamental change in the definition of truth. By this I don't mean that there is no real universe out there and that we simply create whatever kind of reality suits us at the moment. I don't mean that truth is changing in this fashion at all. Instead, the way in which we know the reality out there is changing at an incredible pace. Consider, for a moment, how different the microscopic universe appears when viewed through the old-fashioned microscopes used in high school science classes thirty years ago compared to the view afforded by the most recent high-tech, computer-assisted, electron microscopes. That microscopic universe looks quite different now. The same sort of changing view is now occurring time and again in all sorts of areas, even in our understanding of the Bible. (I'll talk more about this below.) But it isn't simply technology that is giving us a different view of the universe around us; the very paths we use to explore that universe are changing. The advent of cell phones and video texting is drastically changing closed and secretive societies like Myanmar and China. The flow of information and news can no longer be controlled effectively by the central governments of either country, resulting in irreversible social change. Particularly in the case of China, that change will be global in scope. The following observation made by Adam Bly, editor-in-chief of the very thoughtful and future-looking science magazine *Seed*, brings the effects of this change to our focus:

> We are living in a moment where our traditional sources of truth—legacy news outlets, heads of state, community leaders, etc.—have diminished in standing. . . . And we're left having shifted the power equation but desperately lacking new ideas to fill the void that we have revealed. So now what?[1]

The "now what" is doubt. Nothing can be taken for granted anymore. Not just the formulation of *religious* truth, but all sorts of commonly held ideas about politics, education, the global economy, the use of natural resources, energy availability, and just about anything else you might think of are under renewed scrutiny. Bly has put his finger on something very important. The way we make knowledge—the way we know and think about the world around us—is changing. Consequently, doubt.

But this isn't such a bad thing. We doubters take things very seriously—especially the things that are important to us. This serious scrutiny uncovers pretenders with no real substance. The true from the false, the real from the shadow, are revealed, more often than not, as a result of doubters testing the claim or authority to see if it really is so. Doubt can be very uncomfortable, but it can also be very beneficial.

CHANGE IN THE NATURE OF AUTHORITY

A second reason the Bible has been cloaked in doubt has to do with the changing nature of social authority. Conventional authority figures, upon whom we have relied for direction and insight—whether it be scientific, political, or religious—have all suffered a credibility crisis with the resultant rise of popular skepticism and doubt. As religious authorities are diminished in credibility (whether fairly or not), so too the Bible has lost credibility both as a religious authority in its own right and in its use by other religious authorities.

For the past twenty years it has been my job to introduce first-year university students to the Bible. If you find yourself in the group that came of age at the turn of the millennium, let me say directly that the rest of us are watching you with great interest. You are creating a cultural shift with deep significance. The trends that you introduced during your college years are gradually becoming cultural norms as we progress through the first quarter of the twenty-first century. In a manner that has grown in intensity over the past twenty years, you have demonstrated a growing doubt about the Bible, its place within your own lives, and its place within the culture you are creating. But it goes much further than just the Bible. Progressively, you have concluded religion is itself pretty doubtful, and because the Bible is perceived as a religious book, the Bible too has lost its sure footing as an object of respect and trust. In fact, and with good reason, you are sifting out authority figures of all sorts in a challenge to see what will last.

When applied to the Bible, this loss of credible authority works out in several ways. The Bible has been cast into doubt because the claims it makes and the claims made about it are so high and lofty. But doubt about these lofty claims doesn't have to be threatening. If indeed the Bible is a word from God, or even if it is simply a collection of very important writings with a lot of good advice, it ought to be able to withstand the scrutiny that all important things demand. Should the Bible have a significant role to play into the twenty-first century, it will only be as a result of the tangible, pragmatic, and very real help it offers to its readers. Just as any parent discovers all too soon, the rationale "because I said so" isn't very effective. The Bible can no longer claim a special place simply "because I said so" or because a religious leader says so or because some isolated sentence within the Bible says so. If the Bible has a future, it will be because doubters grant it one. It will be because you, the generation of the twenty-first century, have asked your sincere and very hard questions, and it will be because the Bible has emerged from this testing fire with confirmation.

For some of you, the Bible is clouded in a fog of doubt simply because the Bible is a closed book. Many of you have heard about the Bible but have never really spent time reading it, or at best know it only secondhand from movies and novels. Still others have doubts because you have spent time with the Bible, slammed it shut, and have come away shaking your heads at the sometimes outrageous things you've read.

Complicating things all the more is an abundance of religious preachers, teachers, and hawkers of religious "must haves" all claiming to have the final word on the message of the Bible. Even though many claim to proclaim a message "based on the Bible," a great many of these religious authorities are in flat contradiction to the others. Overlay all this with the almost daily barrage of news stories featuring bombings, attempted bombings, shootings, wars, and violence of all sorts motivated, to no small degree, by religious identities that draw the Bible right into the middle of the turmoil. It should be no surprise that Bible doubters are growing in number.

CHANGE IN THE NATURE OF CHRISTIANITY

A third major change that is expressing itself in doubt about the Bible is the change that is occurring in the nature of Christianity. It used to be that Christianity was pretty much defined by people who went to church. The church (all denominations included) was the visible expression of Christianity. This is no longer the case. A rift has occurred separating the church from Christianity, resulting in an ever-growing number of people who define themselves as *de-churched.* The de-churched maintain a vibrant spiritual life and consider themselves Christians, but for whatever reason have not found the church necessary or even helpful. Chances are you consider yourself part of this de-churched group. The de-churched recognize a separation between spirituality and religion that leads us to think about the Bible in whole new ways. Most obviously, this separation between spirituality and religion means that the Bible, as a book about spirituality, doesn't need to be constrained by the interpretations favored by any one religious group, church, or denomination. Church leaders or spokespersons are no longer the recognized authorities on Bible interpretation. Competing voices, sometimes flavored with more than a little sensationalism, attempting to tell the rest of us what the Bible means, have led many to conclude the Bible is a book with no clear voice of its own.

It's not just the de-churched who are forcing a change within Christianity. Christianity is also changing from within in ways that are influencing the churched, the de-churched, and the nonreligious alike. These changes from within are not limited to Christianity and have to do with the way organized religions fit into the larger context of Western culture. The way in which religion in general and Christianity in particular functions to legitimize political positions is changing, with as yet no clear end point in sight. The presidential campaigns that led up to the November 2008 election provide ample illustrations.

In the early spring of 2007, and just prior to his death, Jerry Falwell, founder of the Moral Majority and a leading political activist for fundamentalist Christianity, related an imaginary conversation between a United States Marine and Chelsea Clinton. During the imaginary conversation, the Marine told Chelsea, "There are three things I fear most: Osama, Obama, and your Momma."[2] The force of the statement comes from more than the clever rhyme. Implicit in Falwell's statement is a connection between religion (in this case radical Islam) and political positions at odds with those favored by fundamentalist Christianity. It's unfortunate but not surprising that during the campaigns of the spring and summer of 2008 Barack Obama felt compelled to repeatedly defend himself against two politically motivated accusations: (1) that he is Muslim, and (2) that he is unpatriotic. Religion, nationalism, and a certain brand of family values have long been associated in American culture (God, Mom, and apple pie), but progressively that association is becoming quite explicit and the God of this triad is wearing the garb of fundamentalist Christianity. All of us, Christian and non-Christian alike, would do well to think seriously about the powerful potential religion represents when placed into the political arena.

But there is more. Christianity is a moving target, changing as its environment changes. All the signs point in one direction: Christianity and the way many people view the Bible are about to receive an extreme makeover! That makeover will have a ripple effect leading many to reevaluate their affiliation with organized Christianity. In a nutshell, Christianity has moved south. For most of its history Christianity's day-to-day world was first

European and later North American. This is no longer the case. Christianity has moved south and is beginning to be characterized by ways of thinking about things more at home in the Southern Hemisphere than in the Northern. This move south has resulted in a new Christianity, what Philip Jenkins calls a "distinctive new tradition of Christianity comparable to Catholicism, Protestantism, and Orthodoxy."[3] Christianity has found a new home among the world's poorest.[4] The shift south means more than just a shifting demographic among adherents. Christianity's new home means that there will be changes in theology, ritual, and metaphor—changes in the way of looking at the world though "Christian" eyes—that will have profound implications for the way in which believers view the Bible. Reflect for a moment on the following observation made by Philip Jenkins:

> European Christians reinterpreted the faith through their own concepts of social and gender relations, and then imagined that their culturally specific synthesis was the only correct version of Christian truth. . . . As Christianity moves southward, the religion will be comparably changed by immersion in the prevailing cultures of those host societies.[5]

When most Christians live in non-European cultures, Christianity gets reshaped—reshaped even in its perception and use of the Bible. As one Catholic archbishop observed, "Our Namibian African people have accepted Christ. But this Christ walks too much among them in a European garment."[6] This Christ is about to change wardrobes.

There is another change happening that will affect the dechurched. This trend is not so easy to forecast and this is where it may get scary. Thanks to the Internet we are truly a global community. Right in the middle of this global boiling pot is the international experience of religion. Almost daily the news media reminds us this pot has, more than once, boiled over with terrible consequences.

> Based on recent experiences around the world . . . we face the likelihood that population growth will be accompanied by intensified rivalry, by struggles for converts, by competing attempts to enforce moral codes by means of secular law. . . . Putting these different trends together, we have a volatile mixture that could well provoke appalling wars and confrontations. . . . Worldwide, religious trends have the potential to reshape political assumptions in a way that has not been seen since the rise of modern nationalism.[7]

The emerging global Christendom will have a very different look to it than its twentieth-century predecessor had. Christianity in the twenty-first century will have different issues, which probably will include the global climate change, energy scarcity, and non-state-sponsored as well as state-sponsored violence and terrorism.

How the Bible will be present in the emerging global community is not at all clear, but this much is plain: it will be different. In a later chapter we will examine together some of what this means for those of us who are trying to understand the Bible in the here and now. But for the moment it is enough to simply recognize that change in how the Bible is read and by whom is happening. Consider a second observation made by Philip Jenkins:

> The era of Western Christianity has passed within our lifetimes, and the day of Southern Christianity is dawning. The fact of change itself is undeniable; it has happened, and will continue to happen.[8]

A measure of that change is on our doorstep already. In the north at least, that change is leading to religious doubt. Aspects of the doubt created by that change were made very clear by the *Pew Report on Religion in America*, published in the spring and summer of 2008.[9] As identified by that report, the fastest growing group in America's religious landscape is the religiously unaffiliated.[10] That is, in the United States, formal religious associations are losing their appeal because they are increasingly perceived as unnecessary for gaining entrance to heaven and access to God, or in providing an adequate foundation for moral choices. And when it comes to the Bible, about a third of Christians believe it should be interpreted literally as God's word, about a third say it should not be interpreted literally, and about a quarter of all American adults believe that their own faith's sacred text is not God's word at all.[11] For many the Bible no longer represents a trusted source for religious or spiritual knowledge.

CHANGE IN OUR KNOWLEDGE OF THE BIBLE

A final change that is creating doubt about the Bible is really an application of the previous two changes. What we know about the Bible is changing very quickly. A little earlier we thought together about changing concepts of truth and used as an example of those changes the different views of the microscopic world available when using an old optical microscope as opposed to a new high-tech electron microscope. The vastly improving body of knowledge and clearer resolution now available using the modern devices is analogous to the way in which the field of biblical studies has changed over the past thirty years. Our understanding of the Bible has changed in several ways.

First, the conditions leading to the writing of the individual books of the Bible are much better understood. The dynamics of the oral prehistory resident behind many of the biblical books and the way in which those oral forms transformed into written documents is being investigated afresh with surprising and valuable new insights. Our understanding of how the biblical books were written and why they were written is becoming clearer and clearer.

Second, the manner in which the documents now comprising the Bible were gathered and chosen to be included as sacred text is receiving renewed investigation. Along with the books that are now in the Bible, many other documents were written and used with benefit by the various communities of faith from whom the Bible eventually emerged. Why and how some books were recognized as sacred and placed in the biblical collection is a process even now not fully understood. But as some of those other documents receive renewed attention, either through popular movies

(Mel Gibson's *Passion of the Christ*), through books (*The DaVinci Code*), or through archaeological recovery (the Gospel of Judas),[12] legitimate and serious questions are raised concerning the special status of some books (the ones in the Bible) and the withholding of that status from others. This question of status is not limited to the "lost books" of the Bible. Why shouldn't other sacred books be considered?

Third, ways of interpreting the Bible have changed. This kind of change isn't new. In fact, changing interpretations not subject to a controlling central institution are part and parcel of the Protestant ethos. What is different about the present is the rate and depth of that change.[13] As new technologies confront us with new ethical dilemmas, as globalization and global communication bring a variety of perspectives and cultural norms into our immediate experience, and as a worldwide sense of distrust in authoritative institutions causes people to rethink political and economic sources of stability, the way in which we read the Bible also changes.

SO WHAT ABOUT ME?

I suspect none of us need much convincing that change is occurring. The point of this chapter has simply been to point out the significant and legitimate questions this change raises for our understanding of the Bible. As old certainties give way to new questions, there is reason for doubt. These aspects of deep change are creating complications for the Bible and leading serious people to ask substantial questions about the Bible's continued credibility and value. Doubt is not unreasonable.

But now we need to pause a moment. It's one thing to dispassionately consider evidences for change and the characteristics of the new forms that will emerge, but it's something else altogether to actually experience those changes. The changes are happening in starts and stops, unevenly, and at different times in different places. These changes, in step with new economic realities, energy concerns, and job uncertainties, will have very visible expressions. Denominations built largely around the religious debates of the past will continue to fade or change their identities. Large church programs will encounter mounting economic pressure in the face of a trend toward downsizing. Inevitably, these changes will involve conflict.

Some of you are committed to current forms of religious expression and with good reason will perceive changes as morally wrong and threatening. You will find it a challenge to perceive the transience of cultural forms and will be tempted to conclude the change is an abandonment of "the faith." Others of you are in the camp of the de-churched. You may find yourself thinking "good riddance" to religious forms that simply are unable to communicate any longer or when they do communicate are only intolerant and condemnatory. Conflict, personal attack, and deep hurt will be felt equally by those of you advocating changes and by those of you resisting changes.

Knowing that doubt and conflict often travel together, we will take a lesson. In matters of spirituality and faith, doubt is all too often perceived negatively and can quickly become an occasion for guilt or religious browbeating. We will have none of that. On the journey we are taking together, we will assume that an honest effort to investigate the answers to our questions will lead us to a more accurate understanding and, perhaps, to a deeper and richer experience with God.

We began this chapter by asking a question: does the Bible really matter anymore? It would be easy to answer this question *yes* and cite that the Bible still is a best-selling book, political candidates still drop lines of the Bible into stump speeches, a lot of television preachers talk about it, and soldiers still carry it into war. But does it *really* matter? Or perhaps we ought to rephrase the question: is the Bible relevant in producing a positive impact? The honest answer is: I don't know. I can tell you that the Bible has had a positive impact on me, and later on I'll attempt to explain why and how. But on a larger scale, will the Bible matter and be of help for people in years to come? I don't know. The changes that we are facing in the first quarter of the twenty-first century cannot be minimized, and in the end nobody can truly predict their outcome. What can be said with confidence is that in no small measure the negative or positive impact made by the Bible will be a result of how it is used and by whom. There can be no denying that the Bible has been put to some pretty horrendous as well as some pretty fantastic uses. Moderating those negative applications have been the doubters—people like you and me who are willing to test the authenticity of the mainstream by providing checks and balances, rejecting the extremes. So you see, what we are about as we journey through this book is bigger than any of us individually. The impact the Bible has in the future will be guided by the doubters, those willing to ask the hard questions and test the prevailing wisdom. So, given the importance of the role thrust upon us, we will respect one another's questions and explore together the paths that lie before us.

CHAPTER TWO

DOESN'T THE BIBLE SAY JUST WHAT YOU WANT IT TO SAY?

David Mills, a popular author trying to figure out the relationship between modern science and the Bible, concluded that "interpreting scripture is simply one person's opinion against another's."[1] If that's all it is—one person's opinion against another—what makes one Bible, or the many experts offering insight into its meaning, more credible than all the others? Doesn't the Bible say whatever you want it to say?

Mills's conclusion is reinforced by the way Bibles are presented by those wishing to sell them. I recently received in the mail a couple of catalogs advertising Christian books and curios. I paged through the catalogs to the sections advertising Bibles and was amazed and then bewildered by what I found. The catalogs advertised the Spirit of the Reformation Study Bible, the Bible for Catholics, the Maxwell Leadership Bible, the Evangelical Bible, and the Lutheran Bible; a Bible for women, one for students, a Bible for men, a Bible for teens (including one for Catholic teens), and several children's Bibles; Amplified, Expanded, Revised, and Open Bibles; Hope, Abundant Life, New Spirit-filled Life, and Serendipity Bibles. There was a minister's Bible, a Life Recovery Bible, and an Archaeology Study Bible. There was an Apologetics Study Bible advertised as " 'the thinking person's' edition of God's Word" (implying that other editions are for people who don't think), the NET Bible ("a Bible that explains itself"), the Ancient Faith Bible (allowing readers to "absorb the passion of the early church"), and a Hebrew-Greek Key Word Study Bible by which you can "gain a deeper understanding of God's Word—without having to learn the original languages." I found in another catalog the Surfer's Bible New Testament, which is "designed for surfers by Christian Surfers International," (I suspect that a Christian surfer is a surfer who happens to be a Christian—although I really don't know) and a Backpacker's Bible New Testament. Perhaps most interesting of all there was the One Minute Bible, the 30 Day Bible, the 90 Day Bible, the One Year Bible, and the Lifetime Bible! Each of these different Bibles has a different hook and achieves its distinctiveness through the combination of the particular translation used, combined with introductory notes and reader helps that give a particular slant on the biblical text, and a series of cross-references that make connections between sometimes widely disparate parts of the biblical text. The combination of the translation used and the different add-ons gives each Bible its own particular "feel" or "read" and leads the reader down a specific path in understanding the biblical text.

This wide range of publications, each putting a slightly different slant on the Bible, leads to a quite understandable question: Do all these lenses (Bible for ____; simply fill in the blank) mean that the Bible is a book moldable to special interest groups, all making it fit their own purposes?[2] Is the Bible nothing more than one person's opinion against another's?

TAKING THE BIBLE OUT OF CHURCH

Not so long ago there was a clear line of authority and it was easy to identify the "right" way to interpret the Bible. The Bible belonged in church, and just as the Supreme Court is positioned to tell the rest of us what the Constitution means, church leaders were best positioned to tell the rest of us what the Bible means. Things have changed. The religious landscape in America at the beginning of the twenty-first century is very different than it was in the middle of the twentieth century. Three aspects of that changing religious landscape have direct bearing on how we understand the Bible.

First, the Bible no longer plays such a dominant role in church. The pastor or priest used to be recognized as the resident Bible expert and he or she was the person the rest of us went to in order to find out what the Bible meant. In the 1990s the model of pastor as expert in the sacred text (especially in the evangelical and nondenominational churches) gave way to the model of pastor as CEO and expert in human management. Despite religious rhetoric to the contrary, it is clearly evident that when compared to the place the Bible occupied in similar churches fifty years ago, the Bible has now become eclipsed in its influence. The religious direction or advice contained in many sermons, if analyzed, will be shown to originate from sources more akin to pop psychology, movies, successful business guides, or political platforms—even if presented as based on Bible alone. All too often the Bible has become a sourcebook providing an authoritative voice by which to say whatever you want.

It's an easy thing to do—to make the Bible say what you want it to say. It wouldn't be so bad if the one so interpreting the Bible were aware of it—and honest enough to say so. But usually this isn't the case. Often, the persons reading their own preferences *into* the Bible really think that they are mining the one true meaning *from* the Bible and trying to make the case that the rest of us ought to agree and understand the Bible in the same way. It can be troublesome, if not outright dangerous. For, in all this, the authority of the Bible is used to make authoritative the personal bias or preference of the preacher or teacher. I don't mean *dangerous* as an exaggeration. Recently I've seen preachers use the Bible to command people to "vote with God." I've heard callous and uncaring responses to the victims of the 2004 tsunami in the Indian Ocean, to AIDS victims, and to the homeless based upon "what the Bible says." I've read testimony from pedophile victims that asserted their clergy rapists justified those abuses by quoting Bible verses. These shocking and disturbing pronouncements have convinced me there is no one more potentially dangerous than the one who claims to speak for the Bible. But it is equally true that those speaking for the Bible can be of tremendous help. Sometimes it's hard to separate the good from the bad, the true from the false. But this much is sure: the changing religious landscape around us is characterized by a varied and sometimes dubious use of the Bible.

A second part of that changing religious landscape that has led to a separation of the Bible from the believing community, church, or synagogue is the explosion of new sources of information. It is quite likely that the local bookstore, the Internet, or cable television provide just as much, if not more, information about the Bible than what is available in any church or synagogue. A lot of people are saying a lot of things about the Bible, and most of this conversation is outside the bounds of any faith community or commitment.

A third and very important part of this changing religious landscape leading to the exodus of the Bible from the church is the growing number of us who are *de-churched*. For whatever reason, a growing number of people claiming either the label "Christian" or "follower of Jesus" have opted out of regular church attendance and identification with an organized church group.[3] As more and more of us left the church, we took our Bibles with us. It isn't simply that a number of people have become disenfranchised with the organized church and left. No, it runs deeper. Particularly among those of you in your twenties and thirties, religion and spirituality are no longer necessarily connected.[4] Julia Corbett, a specialist studying religion in America, put it like this: "It is clear . . . that being religious and believing in God do not necessarily mean that people attend church or synagogue. In part, this may have to do with a lack of confidence in organized religion."[5] Many of us no longer regard church, or organized religion in general, as the gatekeeper to the kingdom of heaven. Religious institutions of all sorts have fallen into disrespect and suspicion. This credibility gap has left many wondering: Where do I go to get answers to my questions about the Bible? The Bible is still the best-selling book in

America; it's just that more and more, those of us still reading it are not in church.

So without a clear and unambiguous line of authority telling us what the Bible means, are we left with a condition in which the Bible means whatever we want it to mean? Let me suggest the issue facing us is probably better stated in the form of a second set of questions: Does the reader of the Bible need to hold religious beliefs *about* the Bible prior to a meaningful encounter *with* the Bible? Is there a way to sift through the various religious uses of the Bible to get to the Bible itself? Is the Bible capable of standing on its own? Let's consider these questions by thinking about reading the Bible as a conversation.

READING AS A CONVERSATION

When we read the Bible (or any book, really), we engage in a conversation. You, the reader, are one partner in the dialogue and the pages of the book are the other partner in the conversation. The more you or I know about the person with whom we're talking, the better the conversation and the less likely either will misunderstand the other. The same is true in our reading conversation with the Bible. When you or I or any of us read the Bible, we bring to the conversation a lot of baggage. Past experiences, likes and dislikes, your own way of looking at life, extending even to the level of particular meanings for certain words and the mental images and feelings those words conjure up—all of this comes with you when you begin to read the Bible.

But your partner in the conversation also has baggage. The Bible didn't simply drop out of thin air. Just like you and I are conditioned by where we live and when (and these conditions help make us who we are), so too the Bible is conditioned by when it was written, where, by whom, and for what reason. These facts about the Bible are useful things to know if we are going to understand our partner in this reading conversation.

Some of the debate about the meaning of the Bible is a result of focusing on one partner of this reading conversation to the exclusion of the other. It can be diagrammed like this:

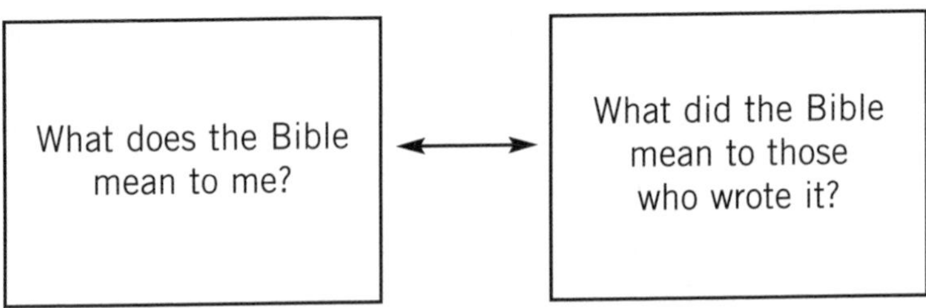

A concentration on the box to the left focuses on you and me, the readers of the Bible. The box on the right seeks to know everything possible about our partner in the reading conversation, the Bible itself. When our reading conversation spotlights one or the other partner in this conversation (the box to the left *or* the box to the right) without equal attention to the other, we increase our chances of misunderstanding. This happens a lot and can be seen in that pressure to hold religious convictions about the Bible before attempting an encounter with the Bible.

Another model is possible, one that seeks to prevent excluding either partner in this conversation. Instead of thinking about the two boxes as separate and distinct from each other, perhaps we ought to see the two in the following manner:

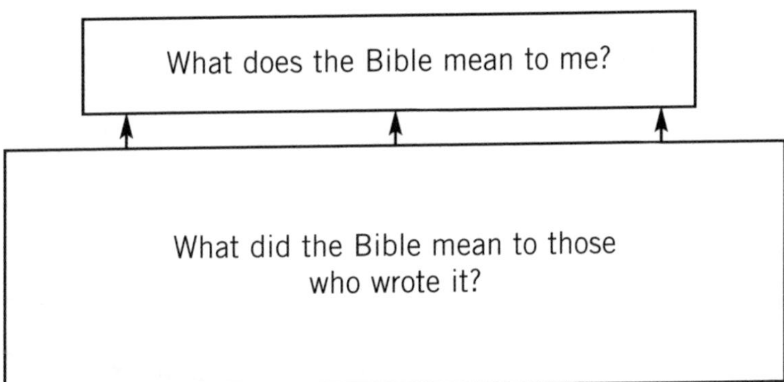

In this model, our understanding of the Bible as it was first written, our partner in the conversation, forms the basis and parameters in answering the question of what it means to me. But as with any conversation, our reading conversation with the Bible is dynamic, lively, and changing. We ask questions, learn more about where our conversation partner is coming from, and in the whole process learn more about ourselves as well. It's not a one–way communication as implied in our second diagram. So perhaps a third model should be considered.

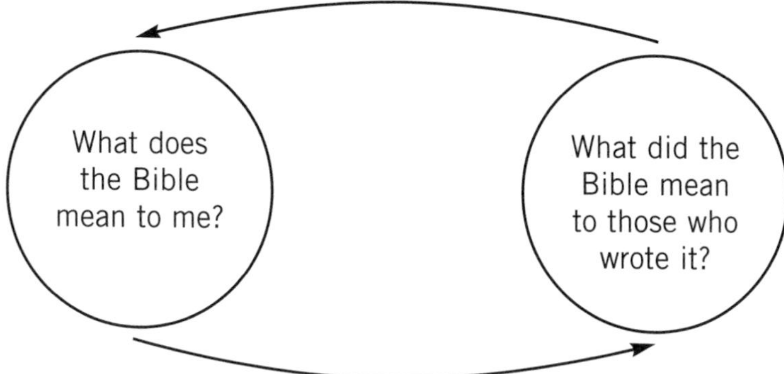

The more we learn about both parties in our reading conversation, the more meaningful our reading can be. Recognizing that this process of learning and conversation is never ending implicitly recognizes that none of us have the final word on what the Bible says. For some that's a difficult pill to swallow.

UNDERSTANDING OUR PLACE IN THE CONVERSATION

This Bible-reading conversation has gone on for a long time. We are only the most recent participants in the conversation and all the twists and turns the Bible-reading conversation has taken over the years influence us now. The same is true in any conversation. Should you enter a room and join a conversation already begun by a couple of your friends, it would be rude to simply jump in with your mouth open. It would be better to listen first and discover what they were talking about. You would then add your own unique contribution to the conversation, but that contribution would most likely fit into the topic and mood of what happened before you arrived. The same is true with the Bible. It is equally rude to think that we read the Bible in a vacuum, isolated from those who have already engaged in the conversation.

THE BIBLE-READING CONVERSATION BEFORE WE ARRIVED

Whether we know it or not, our own reading of the Bible has been influenced by those who have preceded us. Even if it's nothing more than the way the Bible is bound together into a book, divided into chapters and verses, or accompanied by notes in the margins, other Bible readers have left their mark and affect the way we now read the Bible. Knowing that we are jumping into a conversation that began long before we ever joined in makes it easier to understand why there are so many different conclusions about what the Bible means.

Just as you and I are conditioned by the time and place in which we live, so too were those who came before us in this Bible-reading conversation. There have been four great movements or epochs in this conversation since the last of the New Testament books were written, each movement characterized by its own reading paradigm or way of looking at the world around us.[6]

Early Christian Interpretation: Promise-Fulfillment (100–600 C.E.)
Medieval Christian Interpretation: Spiritual-Physical (600–1500 C.E.)
Modern Biblical Interpretation: Objective-Subjective (1500–Present)
Late-Modern Biblical Interpretation: Immediate-? (1970–Present)

Each of these movements, spanning hundreds of years, operated according to its own rules and made use of its own peculiar way of looking at reality. People in each of these time periods interpreted the Bible in a manner that made sense at that time. Occasionally, the way that the New Testament authors understood the Old Testament books appears to us in the twenty-first century as rather strange and sometimes flat wrong. That's because those New Testament writers, when compared to us today, had a different way of looking at the world around them and so found meanings in the Old Testament texts that appear quite strange to us.

The writers of the New Testament considered Jesus the fulfillment of divine promises made in the past. In order to use the Old Testament as information about Jesus, a typological method of interpretation was used by the writers of the New Testament when referring to, quoting, or alluding to the material contained in the Old Testament. The New Testament writers found in the pages of the Old Testament typological pointers that enabled them to understand and interpret the life, death, and resurrection of Jesus.

The writer of Matthew made liberal use of material taken from the Hebrew Bible in presenting Jesus as the fulfillment of the Hebrew Bible tradition (see Matthew 1:22; 2:15, 17, 23; 4:14; 8:17; 12:17; 13:14, 35; 21:4; 27:9). A contemporary reader who bothers to retrace Matthew's references will be left quite bewildered because the various Old Testament passages Matthew refers to seem to have nothing to do with Jesus; they speak about other topics altogether. Further, Matthew isn't very careful about what he's doing when referring to those Old Testament texts that are being fulfilled. Matthew conflates Old Testament texts (Matthew 21:4 conflating Isaiah 62:11 and Zechariah 9:9; Matthew 27:9 conflating Zechariah 11:12-13 and Jeremiah 18:1-3); changes those texts either in wording or in meaning (Matthew 2:15 in reference to Jesus even though the quoted text, Hosea 11:1, has the nation of Israel in mind); and even credits a phrase to the Old Testament, even though that phrase is nowhere to be found in the Old Testament—at least as we know it today (Matthew 2:23 where Matthew uses the term *Nazarene*, whereas the closest Old Testament text is Isaiah 11:1 using the similar-sounding Hebrew word for *branch*). For Matthew, it seems to be enough that we as readers get the general idea. He wasn't hung up on getting it just right, either when quoting the Old Testament text word for word or even when assigning the Old Testament text to the right book or author. For the writer of the Gospel of Matthew, variations in how the Old Testament biblical text was presented were totally acceptable.

More examples can be found. The writer of Luke recounts an episode of the resurrected Jesus walking unrecognized with several dispirited disciples, and along their journey he explains to them the meaning of the events that had recently occurred.

> And he said to them, "O foolish men, and slow of heart to believe all that the prophets have spoken! Was it not necessary that the Christ should suffer these things and enter into his glory?" And beginning with Moses and all the prophets, he interpreted to them in all the scriptures the things concerning himself. (Luke 24:25-27)

The way that Luke presents it, Jesus found plenty of references to himself in these centuries-old texts—you just had to know how to look.

The writer of the New Testament book of Hebrews does the same thing. Quoting liberally from a variety of sources within the Hebrew Bible tradition, the writer of Hebrews uses all of these ancient texts to explain their fulfillment in the person of Jesus. Chapter 1 of Hebrews alone strings together seven different references (Psalm 2:7; 2 Samuel 7:14; Deuteronomy 32:43; Psalm 104:4; Psalm 45:6-7; Psalm 102:25-27; and Psalm 110:1), applying them to Jesus in one form or another. Chapter 1 is only the beginning! The writer of Hebrews takes text after text from the Hebrew Bible tradition to point the reader to a greater reality seen only vaguely and sometimes in shadow form by those writers of the Old Testament but which is now made plain in the person and work of Jesus.

This typological method of interpretation was not limited to the writers of the New Testament; it became a dominant method of interpretation among other early Christian writers as well. This method of interpretation allowed the reader to make connections to the events and meanings surrounding Jesus, which were otherwise not found in the biblical texts themselves. Undergirding this typological interpretation is the assumption that the older text (the Old Testament) has a fundamental connection to later events (Jesus' life, death, and resurrection) and as such the Old Testament text has within it a dimension of meaning that can only be seen from the perspective of those later events. Peter makes plain use of this method of interpretation when he uses a passage from Joel 2:28-32 to explain the disruptive events happening around him in Jerusalem, recorded in Acts 2. In using the older text to interpret a later event, Peter is free to change the apparent original meaning of the Joel text, for in Joel *all flesh* (2:28) is clearly limited to the Jewish people, whereas in Peter's use of the same reference (Acts 2:5-21; especially v. 17) *all flesh* means all nations—going far beyond ethnic Jews. The typological method of interpretation is not so much interested in what the texts meant to those who wrote them but rather is interested in discovering what those texts now mean in light of later events (Jesus) and understandings.

But this way of looking at the Bible changed, and changed again, as the years went by. The promise-fulfillment paradigm gave way to other dominant ways of thinking about the biblical books and different meanings were gleaned from the pages of the Bible.

STANDING AT THE CROSSROADS

The periods of the Bible-reading conversation change when the fundamental ideas about the nature of reality, generally accepted by most people, begin to falter and change into something else. The change from one period to another doesn't happen overnight and the transition from one to another is difficult, involving questions and doubts about all sorts of previously accepted ideas. Most believe we are in one of those transition periods right now.

If we are living through a period of transition, and I think we are, it will have important implications for how we understand the Bible. First, bear in mind that Bible interpretation takes place within the confines of how *truth* is defined at any particular time—and that definition changes. In chapter 1, we saw that the changing perception of truth is one of the chief characteristics of the change we are currently experiencing on a global scale. Second, transitions of this kind don't occur overnight. We are at a meeting point where two dominant paradigms (the Modern and the Late-Modern) for interpreting the Bible are competing and sometimes conflicting. As a result, it should come as no surprise that there are wide varieties of Bible interpretation now being offered. It should also come as no surprise that doubt is the result. We are standing at a crossroads that will take years to sift out.

In the Modern period of biblical interpretation, the goal was to understand the author's intended communication within the scope of the written text. The Modern period sought out objective information to uncover what the author of a particular biblical text meant when he or she wrote that text. The guiding question for the Modern period is: what did the author mean?

In the Late-Modern period the question is: what are we to make of this text? Those operating in the Late-Modern paradigm contend that there is no hope of, nor is it even desirable to try, entering the "world of the author," for we are locked within our own world defined by our own circumstance, space, and time. Those reading the Bible under the paradigm of the Late-Modern period realize that the biblical text is now part of our world, not the world of some author of long ago, and our job is to encounter this present text much as we would a painting or other piece of fine art and to appreciate the way the text has helped form the world of the reader. This isn't always a pleasant experience, for just as some pieces of art have a shocking and disturbing effect and other pieces of art give unmistakable signs of participating in prejudice, economic oppression, and violence, so too the Late-Modern reader understands the Bible has all too often been a willing accomplice in some of the uglier moments of human history. The history of the Bible's use has given platform to the oppression of women and the divinely sanctioned genocide of whole ethnic groups. The history of the Bible's use is now unalterably part of the text itself. Yet, just as with art, in which there is no one *correct* interpretation, the Late-Modern reader approaches the biblical text not *just* to find one uniform authoritative direction (in fact authorities of all sorts are often met with distrust) but to *also* find a fertile field of possibilities for enriching the present, new ways of describing our own experiences and, at times, a means of critiquing the Bible's role in forming the present.

If in the Modern period the text provided a bridge allowing communication between the ancient author and the contemporary reader, the Late-Modern interpreter seeks a conversation with the text itself, understanding that it is the text that is present to the contemporary reader and not the ancient author. In this conversation between text and reader, the reader brings just as much to the dialogue as does the text. Interpretation is as much an understanding of the reader as it is an understanding of the text.

This idea of self-understanding when reading a text was brought forcefully home to me several months ago. A friend of mine let me borrow his copy of a book I wrote on heaven. I was amazed to see what sentences he underlined, wrote notes next to, and highlighted as the most important ideas. Often the sections he marked were not the ones I would have highlighted. They were not the sentences that I thought were the most important and were not the sentences that meant the most to me. It was clear that my friend had engaged in a conversation first with the book and only second with me, the author of the book. His highlights were altogether appropriate, for they marked out ideas that were of importance to him at that time and at that particular place in his life. As I observed my friend reading the book, I learned as much about him as I did about the book. When reading the book, my friend was asking: What is here for me? And that's not a bad idea.

But does all this talk about periods of interpretation and paradigms and ways of reading mean that those of us who simply want to try to read the Bible and make sense of it are on a fool's errand? Are we simply wrong to think that the Bible has something to say to us that is more than a way of reading or a meaning we unwittingly place into the Bible? No, I don't think so. Part of the strength and, in my opinion, the appeal of the Bible is that it can communicate to us right where we are, at this time in history, and at this place. The Bible does have a voice of its own and we can learn to listen to that voice.

PULLING IT ALL TOGETHER: SOME PRACTICAL SUGGESTIONS

We've spent enough time thinking together about this Bible-reading conversation. It's now time to pursue practical steps in making the conversation meaningful. The suggestions that follow are meant as guides, not rules that must be observed if the Bible is to be usefully read.

1. BEGIN AT THE BEGINNING

a. What do we know about the author and the circumstances of the text?

Literature—including the literature that finally made its way to become the Bible—is written for a purpose. Someone wrote the books of the Bible to someone for some purpose, and as a beginning point in understanding the Bible it is important to understand something of the person who wrote the literature and why he wrote. Here's an example. Suppose you're reading along and come across the following sentence: *There will be no classes tomorrow*. If you are a student in school, the sentence is good news—very good news. It means you get a day off and probably have an opportunity to catch up on some much-needed sleep! If Principal Smith (or some other obviously important school official) wrote the sentence, our hunches are confirmed and the party begins! If, however, Karl Marx signed the sentence, then the statement "There will be no classes tomorrow" means something else altogether. No matter how hard we try, we simply won't be able to wring a day away from school out of the sentence. Knowing the purpose for the sentence makes all the difference in the world in understanding the sentence correctly. But this very fundamental idea has been quite frequently cast aside when it comes to the Bible. If the interpretation of the Bible is separated from the meaning of the original author, then anything goes.

A clear and in my mind very sad example of separating the words of the Bible from their original meaning can be found in Luke 21:1-3. In this passage Jesus comments on the sacrifice made by a poor widow as she contributed two coins to the temple treasury. Many have used this passage to applaud the woman and to encourage others to sacrificial giving to a church when, in reality—and as the verses preceding in Luke 20:45-47 make clear—Jesus is pronouncing quite strong condemnation on those who would devour widow's houses by encouraging such a contribution! The author's intention in the Luke passage was just the opposite of how it is now most often used.

b. What kind of text are you reading?

An appreciation of the type of literature being read is an important step in understanding the literature. A simple example will illustrate. When reading a cartoon in the local newspaper and coming across the name "Doonesbury," I am prepared to understand the name as referring to a fictional character because I understand I'm reading a cartoon. Moreover, because I know the style of cartoon that Doonesbury represents, I am prepared to understand the statements and dialogue in the cartoon as a form of irony and political satire. If, however, I read the name "Mr. Doonesbury" in the article on the front page of that same newspaper, I am prepared to understand Mr. Doonesbury as a real, live person who spoke words that could be recorded on a tape recorder or who acted in a manner that could be captured on a video recorder. The names could be exactly the same or the statements could be exactly the same in the cartoon as in the front page article, yet because I know the difference between a cartoon and a news article, I am prepared to understand those names and speeches quite differently. In fact, if I tried to understand the cartoon as a news article or the news article as a cartoon, I would botch things very badly. Just as newspapers include all sorts of different types of literature (news articles, cartoons, advertisements, editorials), so too does the Bible.

One of the most frequent causes for confusion and disagreement in understanding the Bible is a total disregard for the particular kind of writing being examined (epic, song, narrative, letter, prophetic drama). The prophet Joel provides a good example. In Joel 2:31 we read: "The sun shall be turned to darkness, and the moon to blood." It would be strange indeed if we completed the sentence: "and the rest of the country will be sunny and mild." I think everyone would see the completion of the sentence as pure nonsense—the Joel prophecy is not a weather report! Joel provides an easily understood example of literary confusion. But what about Job or Jonah? Are they real persons whose stories are recorded as though in a news article? Or are they more like Sherlock Holmes, fictional characters constructed to communicate really important ideas? Or are they a mix, real news-article-like people who have been now incorporated into fictional stories with important lessons to teach?[7]

2. THE RIPPLE EFFECT

It is a constant temptation to interpret one biblical text by importing meaning from another biblical text. Unless the writer of the text in question also refers back to the second biblical text, this method of importing meaning from one to another is a suspect method at best and often leads to mistaken conclusions. Instead, think of interpretation as ripples on a pond. Start with the immediate context of the passage in question, move to the broader context of the particular book in which the passage is found, and only finally to related biblical books that might have exerted an influence on the writer in question. The argument that the Bible was all written by God and so can with validity all be interchanged when seeking out what a particular part means is a slippery slope that often is only limited by the ingenuity of the preacher or television evangelist seeking to make the Bible say what he or she would prefer it to say. If the individual parts of the Bible are removed from their own particular historical contexts, they can be made to mean just about anything. And if they mean just about anything, they mean nothing.

3. READ SLOWLY

Let's face it. The Bible is a hard book. It's not the place to practice your speed-reading skills. The Bible is best read slowly. Think of the Bible as a poem or an anthology of short stories, tightly woven, where words are used very carefully. Pay attention to the structure of the sentences and to the preference for one word over another by a particular biblical author. To benefit most by reading slowly, it will be useful to consider the kind of translation you are reading. Translations reside on a spectrum with what is called a dynamic translation on one end and a static translation on the other.

Dynamic____Static

A dynamic translation attempts to capture the sense of the original text, freely modifying the structure, grammar, and syntax of the original in order to provide a more readable translation. On the other end of the spectrum, static translations tend to pay close attention to the structure, grammar, and vocabulary of the original text and as much as possible replicate those details in the translation, even if the result is a translation that seems more wooden and less readable. Although translations tend to one end of the spectrum or the other, they aren't always consistent, and within one translation there will be parts that are more dynamic and other parts that are more static. Here is an example of the value of reading a static translation slowly.

Good Hebrew prose will often introduce the subject of the narrative in the beginning of the story. The following verbs that involve the subject use pronouns and usually don't repeat the subject. The pattern is presented in the New American Bible (NAB) translation of Exodus 2:23b-25: "As their cry for release went up to God, he heard their groaning and was mindful of his covenant with Abraham, Isaac and Jacob. He saw the Israelites and knew." Notice that the subject *God* appears only at the beginning of the sequence and the verbs *heard, was mindful, saw,* and *knew* are associated with the pronoun *he* or have the pronoun implied. This is the usual pattern for Hebrew prose and is here presented by the NAB in a very readable English translation. Compare it, however, to the same passage presented by the Revised Standard Version (RSV): "Their cry under bondage came up to God. And God heard their groaning, and God remembered his covenant with Abraham, with Isaac, and with Jacob. And God saw the people of Israel, and God knew their condition." In this translation, the subject *God* is repeated with every verb. This translation preserves the pattern provided in the Hebrew original and is just as bad Hebrew as it is English! But that's the point. Just as a writer or speaker might use bad grammar in order to make the reader or listener take note—"Ain't that right!"—the writer of Exodus 2 uses the very same technique—emphasizing the powerful presence of God in the story. Like a hammer striking, or a fist pounding a lectern, the repetition of *God, God, God, God* emphasizes that everything about to happen in the story from this point on is a result of God's powerful presence. The Exodus is God's doing! The RSV presents a static translation preserving the rhetorical design of the original Hebrew writer, whereas the NAB presents a more readable English translation but misses the point.

Reading a reputable static translation (the RSV is probably the best Old Testament and New Testament in English, while the Jewish Publication Society [JPS] provides a very good English translation of the Hebrew Bible) can result in a rich new appreciation of the Bible.

4. READ ALONE AND READ IN A GROUP

Earlier I suggested that reading the Bible is like entering a conversation. At that point, we were talking about how important it is to know something about the person with whom you are talking so as to better understand *where they are coming from*, what they mean by saying certain things, and why they might make those statements. Now it's time to consider the other partner in that conversation. Each of us reads within the context of our own experiences, values, and outlooks, and it can be very helpful to be mindful of the baggage that we bring to our reading of the Bible. It's important to read alone. Just as a private conversation with a good friend can be rich and rewarding, so too reading the Bible on your own can allow you to stop and consider the Bible-reading conversation very personally, within the context of your own life experience. These kinds of readings can be *formative*, a result of the biblical text speaking to you.

But take care not to become unbalanced. We all need to also read in groups. Reading in a group will remind us that others read out of their own experiences, and in fact some of the Bible may have more in common with other life settings than it does with yours or mine. This was brought home to me very powerfully several years ago. I was in eastern Africa during a time of civil unrest and war. For many people it was a desperate time, filled with violence and uncertainty. To my surprise, I discovered that one of the most popular books among people there at that time was the book of Revelation. I admit that book has always been difficult for me and I never really bought into the *Apocalypse Now* model, seeing in the book of Revelation Apache helicopters and nuclear bombs. So I was not prepared for how important the book had become to these people at that time in eastern Africa—but I should have been! People facing an uncertain future wrote the book of Revelation for people facing an uncertain future. It is a book of hope—and those in that war-torn region knew very well the value of hope. They resonated with the book of Revelation more than I, at that point in my life, ever could, for they knew firsthand the conditions experienced by Revelation's author and identified with his offer of a glorious future. I benefited by a group reading of Revelation that offered to me a glimpse of the book's true value. If I had allowed my previously *formative* reading of Revelation to become *normative* for the group reading of Revelation, I would have missed the whole point of the book. I needed the group to hold my own perspective in check and provide corrective and expanding perspectives. Read the Bible alone and benefit from its formative influences, but take care that you resist making those formative influences normative for others. Read alone and read in a group.

5. PRACTICE HUMILITY

In our reading of the Bible, none of us should think that we have the final word, but that shouldn't stop us from the journey. Just because you or I may not be a famous firebrand preacher or a well-published biblical scholar, that doesn't mean we shouldn't even read the Bible at all. I'm not a brain surgeon, but that doesn't stop me from taking an aspirin for my headache. I act on what I do know and seek out the help of others when confronted with what I don't know. The key seems to be in knowing our own limitations and in being willing to seek out input from others who may be of help. If nothing else, reading the Bible requires a good dose of humility.

6. TRANSLATION BY COMMITTEE

All kinds of people produce Bibles and those people are usually identified in the introduction or preface pages that appear right at the beginning of the book. Occasionally, a Bible is produced that reflects the work of one person dominant in the translation or interpretive notes that may accompany the actual biblical text. Generally, it's wise to shy away from these Bibles. Instead, look for a Bible that was translated by a committee, preferably a committee whose members reflect diversity in race, geography, gender, and religion (admittedly, it's hard to tell sometimes just from looking at the information in the introduction). This diversity will add a degree of check and balance to the work of the committee and prevent or at least minimize the imposition of a lens or filter through which the Bible is presented. And if you want to go a step further, keep two or three Bibles produced by different committees handy so you can do your own comparison. No one has the final word, and so it's wise to listen to a variety of voices when attempting to make a go of what the Bible is all about.

7. THE NOTES ARE JUST THE NOTES

In many Bibles, scattered throughout the book, either right before each of the individual books in the Bible or at the bottom of the page or in the side margins, will be notes. These notes attempt to help explain parts of the Bible that are difficult to understand or in some other fashion give to the reader background information about that part of the Bible. Often this information can be very helpful. But remember: the notes are just the notes. Sometimes these notes reflect the idiosyncrasies or religious preferences of the editor. Sometimes the notes are out-of-date and may in fact be misleading or simply wrong in the background information provided about specific parts of the Bible. The point is, recognize that the notes were good-faith attempts to help the reader and may in fact provide a great deal of help, but these notes are not free of mistakes and should always be taken as helpful hints and not as the final word.

8. BE SURPRISED BY WHAT YOU FIND

The old adage "You often find what you're looking for" applies to the Bible as well. Just about every Christian religious group can trot out favorite Bible verses to support its own position or preference when discussing some social issue or other, even if those positions are diametrically opposed to the other group's positions! Unfortunately, disastrous consequences can follow when the resulting "Bible message" is given the authority of

God's word for today when in reality that message had nothing to do with the Bible but originated only from the mind of the interpreter! Hate crimes of all sorts and the fleecing of viewing audiences by televangelists are only two of the many examples that come to mind. But what about you and me? How can we in our own Bible reading escape this trap of reading into the Bible those very things we claim to get out of the Bible?

Being aware of the danger is the first step and being willing to be surprised is the second step in avoiding this trap. Ask yourself this: when was the last time you were taken aback, shocked, or amazed by what you read in the Bible? If the Bible holds no surprise for you it may be simply because you are actually and only looking at a reflection of yourself when you open the pages of the Bible. If you then grant that reflection of yourself the authority of the "word of God," you have become self-deceived to an extent that is truly to be pitied. The lasting value of the Bible has been because of its (sometimes unnerving) ability to change people. The message of the Bible reaches out and makes the reader different. That message is muted, however, when we, knowingly or unknowingly, seek in the Bible only that which affirms what we already believe or are. The message of the Bible is freed when we make ourselves vulnerable, when we allow ourselves to be surprised.

9. BY THEIR FRUIT YOU WILL KNOW THEM

Let me suggest this test to help guide your reading. If indeed the Bible is worth the time and effort, it ought to have a positive impact on those who bother to spend time with it. And so, is it having good fruit? Perhaps unexpected—and often disturbing—the fruit that the Bible produces may not be what we were looking for, but it should be what we need. If the Bible is somehow or other connected with the "word of God" (and we'll look at that connection a bit later), there ought to be positive and visible results for having spent time reading it. That doesn't mean that every time you open the book inspirational warmth will result or a deep insight will be clear (although that does happen sometimes). But over the long haul, things to think about will confront you and, as often as not, these things will change you.

WANT TO KEEP GOING?

The last two bits of advice bring me to a confession that I can no longer avoid. Before you go much further down this path leading you into the Bible, be warned. I've found the Bible to be a dangerous book. In fact, I've found that it becomes most dangerous when I read it most fairly. When I honestly attempt to let it speak for itself and do not impose my own grid of preferences over it—when I have made myself vulnerable to it—it has changed me. Sometimes that change has been welcome and comforting. Sometimes the change has not been pleasant at all.

A little earlier in this chapter I raised several questions: Does the reader of the Bible need to hold religious beliefs *about* the Bible prior to a meaningful encounter *with* the Bible? Is there a way to sift through the various religious uses of the Bible to get to the Bible itself? Is the Bible capable of standing on its own?

I would like to now address those questions in a very direct fashion. In the late 1980s I made a decision that I thought at the time was fairly simple and insignificant. I determined that I would form my religious beliefs based upon what I read in the Bible. I would try to have an encounter with the Bible independent of religious convictions about the Bible. That is, the Bible would shape my religion, and as much as was possible, my religion would not dictate my reading of the Bible. In the years since that decision I've discovered that it was not at all an easy path to choose. In fact, it's been painful. Yet at the same time it's been extremely rewarding. I could never have guessed how my values and priorities were going to be changed and how important the people in my life would become to me. That little statement "Love the Lord your God . . . [and] your neighbor as yourself" (Matthew 22:37-39) has a way of causing all sorts of very deep priority revisions. But there is a downside. Some of the religious ideas I once held tightly are no longer so dear and some people in those religious circles now view me with suspicion and distrust—all of which I could never have imagined in the late 1980s. The point being, yes, it is possible to have an encounter with the Bible without previously forming religious beliefs about the Bible. When we are willing to hold our religious beliefs in suspension, we are most open to reading the Bible as it really is.

The adventure of reading the Bible is never complete. We are all limited by our own circumstances and the moment in history we find ourselves. This recognition doesn't mean the message of the Bible is forever lost and that any interpretation is as good as the next. No, not at all! The recognition of our limitations does not provide an excuse for laziness. Instead, the recognition of our own limitations allows us to come to the Bible expectantly, knowing that at any moment something new may be in store for us. If we refuse to be drawn into the trap that lulls us into thinking we have the final and absolute word on what the Bible says, our reading adventure can be exciting and fresh. A bit earlier I suggested a diagram that may serve as a model for our Bible reading.

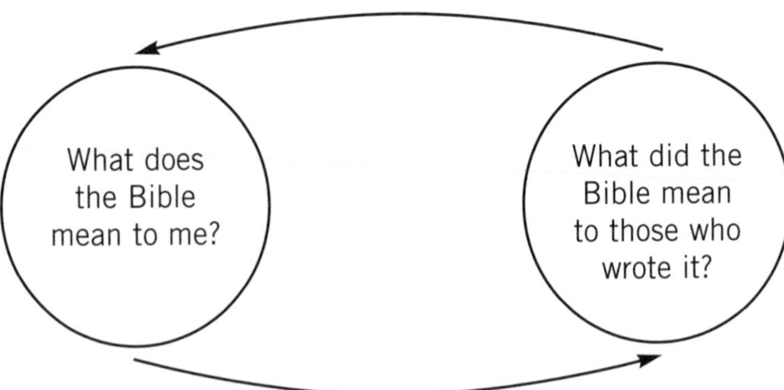

Paying attention to both partners in our reading conversation, understanding the baggage we as readers bring to the conversation, and learning all we can about the Bible as it really is allows us to hear from the Bible more than the echo of our own voices. The suggestions I presented in the previous pages are intended as a beginning in listening to that voice from the Bible.

I've discovered the Bible is quite able to stand on its own. But be warned. As the diagram above suggests, if you choose to make yourself vulnerable to the Bible in this way, you too may be changed in ways that you do not anticipate. It's not easy, but it is worth the ride! If you're still willing, let's see what else might be in store.

CHAPTER THREE

DOES ANYBODY HAVE THE *REAL* BIBLE?

If there is only one Bible, why are Jewish, Protestant, Roman Catholic, and Orthodox Bibles all so different? How in the world can anyone claim the Bible has authority, influence, or simply religious clout when we can't even settle on how the book should read? Is there any way to figure out which is the *real* Bible? The problem is not hypothetical or merely academic. It's a maddening reality encountered by anyone looking at any two Bibles side by side. They don't read the same! Even if we could wade through all the overlay placed on the Bible by its various users (the interpretive matters we discussed in the last chapter), a troublesome reality remains. The number, order, and content of books in the Bibles used by different religious groups are different from one another. So which one is right? If there is considerable variation between Bibles—and there is—it's a fair question to ask. Which Bible is the *real* Bible? We'll break the question down into two parts.

The first part of the question has to do with the books that make up the Bible. Even if we could get back to what was first written, how would we know if the books that are now in the Bible are the ones that should be in the Bible? How, and by whom, were some books chosen to be in the Bible and other books not chosen? Did the people compiling the Bible have their personal agendas at work in this selection that biased the choices of which books to include in the Bible? Is the Bible slanted in some way or other by the choices these people made? What makes these books so special? Are the books bound between the covers of our modern-day Bibles still the pick of the litter?

The second part of the question about which Bible is the real Bible will address the different translations used by different Bibles. Why are there so many different translations and versions of those early books that make up the Bible? Were those books really so difficult to translate? Do the Bibles we have today resemble at all what the Bible was like when it was first written? Why can't people today agree on how to translate the books of the Bible?

HOW WERE THE BOOKS IN THE BIBLE CHOSEN?

As is clear from the series of questions from above, the question concerning the *real* Bible is tied up with the history of the Bible and ultimately pushes us back to ask where the Bible came from. Without doubt, a lot of books were written (including the so-called lost books of the Bible) and circulated at the same time the books of the Bible were written. So why were some of these books collected together, put into the Bible, and labeled "sacred" when others were not? When we begin digging around in the reasons the Bible looks the way it does, it's not long before we must confront serious questions about the agendas of those people who played important roles in shaping the Bible. In all this, the bottom line is: is the Bible simply the product of a biased and narrow viewpoint expressed by the powerbrokers of the day?

Let's think it through. If somebody with a particular goal in mind didn't put the Bible together, the alternative is that the Bible simply fell out of the sky. Although nobody actually says it, at least in so many words, the difficulties posed by a serious look at how the Bible was formed lead many people to come very close to the "fell out of the sky" view of the Bible. Consider the following: "Though I am writing about the Old Testament, 'the Bible Jesus read,' I feel neither qualified nor inclined to delve into such matters as author [or] date of composition."[1] With these words, Philip Yancey begins his popular and award-winning book on the Old Testament, *The Bible Jesus Read*. Unfortunately, it wasn't. The Old Testament wasn't the Bible Jesus read. The truth is that the Old Testament contained in your Bible (and Yancey's) is quite different from the Bible Jesus read. By dismissing this reality of history, Yancey treats the Bible as if it fell from the sky and so avoids those very inconvenient questions of the Bible's reliability that are raised when we go poking around in matters of the Bible's origins.

It's a fair, honest, and important question to ask where the Bible came from. For, if the Bible originated from *within* human history and was not deposited *into* human history, the circumstances of the Bible's origin must have left an indelible mark on the Bible. If the Bible originated from within human history, it is highly probable that its formation involved the same kind of power struggles, positioning, and biases that have gone into the development of every important document. It's often been said that history is written by the winners. Maybe this is true with the Bible as well. If so, how the Bible originated and was passed from one generation to another certainly influences our own determinations about its credibility.

Although we probably will never know the motivations of all the people involved with the Bible's formation, we can at least answer the "from within human history" or "dropped into human history" debate. We can trace the Bible's footprints back pretty far and a lot of clues are left to tell us how the Bible was formed. We need to follow those clues because if the Bible is valuable, it is valuable on its own terms—as it really is—and not the way we would like it to be. So where did the Bible come from? It's a question that has to do with a lot more than just author and date of composition. It's a question that will influence the credibility we grant to the book.

HEBREW BIBLE AND CHRISTIAN OLD TESTAMENT

In our search for the Bible's beginning, we need to break things down a bit. There are two main sections to the Bible, and although now joined, they weren't always. The first part of the Bible, the Christian Old Testament, makes up roughly two-thirds of the Bible and is very similar to the Hebrew Bible used by Judaism.

The Hebrew Bible, as we know it today, is the end result of a long process of writing and sifting out. Many of the books in the Hebrew Bible began orally, passed from one person to another and from one generation to another in the form of stories, songs, tales, and instructions that were spoken and remembered simply because they were so popular and inviting. In its present form, the Hebrew Bible is structured in three large sections: Torah (Instruction), Nevi'im (Prophets), and Kethuvim (Writings).

HEBREW BIBLE

Torah (Instruction)	*Nevi'im (Prophets)*	*Kethuvim (Writings)*
• Genesis • Exodus • Leviticus • Numbers • Deuteronomy	Former Prophets • Joshua • Judges • Samuel (1 and 2) • Kings (1 and 2) Later Prophets • Isaiah • Jeremiah • Ezekiel • *The Twelve* (Hosea, Joel, Amos, Obadiah, Jonah, Micah, Nahum, Habakkuk, Zephaniah, Haggai, Zechariah, Malachi)	• Psalms • Proverbs • Job • Song of Solomon • Ruth • Lamentations • Ecclesiastes (Qohelet) • Esther • Daniel • Ezra • Nehemiah • Chronicles (1 and 2)

The books now contained in these three sections were composed over long periods of time and recognized as part of a sacred collection in quite distinct settings and circumstances. As you can see from the chart below, the order of books and the way they are grouped together is not the same in the Hebrew Bible as in the Christian Old Testament (we'll consider the differences between the Roman Catholic Old Testament and the Protestant Old Testament in a little bit). Those differences are important and figure into the process by which each collection became sacred for different communities of religious faithful.

Hebrew Bible	Roman Catholic Old Testament	Protestant Old Testament
Torah (Instruction)	**Pentateuch**	**Pentateuch**
• Genesis	• Genesis	• Genesis
• Exodus	• Exodus	• Exodus
• Leviticus	• Leviticus	• Leviticus
• Numbers	• Numbers	• Numbers
• Deuteronomy	• Deuteronomy	• Deuteronomy
Nevi'im (Prophets)	**Historical Books**	**Historical Books**
Former Prophets	• Joshua	• Joshua
• Joshua	• Judges	• Judges
• Judges	• Ruth	• Ruth
• Samuel (1 and 2)	• 1 Samuel	• 1 Samuel
• Kings (1 and 2)	• 2 Samuel	• 2 Samuel
Later Prophets	• 1 Kings	• 1 Kings
• Isaiah	• 2 Kings	• 2 Kings
• Jeremiah	• 1 Chronicles	• 1 Chronicles
• Ezekiel	• 2 Chronicles	• 2 Chronicles
• The Twelve (*Hosea,*	• Ezra	• Ezra
Joel, Amos, Obadiah,	• Nehemiah	• Nehemiah
Jonah, Micah,	• Tobit	• Esther
Nahum, Habakkuk,	• Judith	**Poetical Books**
Zephaniah, Haggai,	• Esther	• Job
Zechariah, Malachi)		• Psalms

<table>
<tr>
<td>Kethuvim (Writings)
• Psalms
• Proverbs
• Job
• Song of Solomon
• Ruth
• Lamentations
• Ecclesiastes (Qohelet)
• Esther
• Daniel
• Ezra
• Nehemiah
• Chronicles (1 and 2)</td>
<td>• 1 Maccabees
• 2 Maccabees
Wisdom Books
• Job
• Psalms
• Proverbs
• Ecclesiastes
• Song of Songs (Song of Solomon)
• Wisdom
• Sirach (Ecclesiasticus)
Prophetical Books
• Isaiah
• Jeremiah
• Lamentations
• Baruch
• Ezekiel
• Daniel
• Hosea
• Joel
• Amos
• Obadiah
• Jonah
• Micah
• Nahum
• Habakkuk
• Zephaniah
• Haggai
• Zechariah
• Malachi</td>
<td>• Proverbs
• Ecclesiastes
• Song of Solomon
Prophetical Books
• Isaiah
• Jeremiah
• Lamentations
• Ezekiel
• Daniel
• Hosea
• Joel
• Amos
• Obadiah
• Jonah
• Micah
• Nahum
• Habakkuk
• Zephaniah
• Haggai
• Zechariah
• Malachi</td>
</tr>
</table>

THE IDEA OF A SACRED COLLECTION AND THE FACT OF A SACRED COLLECTION

The *idea* of a collection of sacred books took centuries to develop and was a necessary step before any particular writings were gathered together. There are traces of this idea of sacred books in the Old Testament itself, but those traces did not blossom into the *fact* of a sacred collection until the last several centuries B.C.E. and into the first centuries C.E. The process involved substantial disagreement between competing social groups over which books belonged in the collection and resulted in different collections of sacred books for different groups. Collections of authoritative and sacred texts did not appear in a vacuum but were authoritative and sacred for *someone*. The history of the formation of the Bible is intricately wound up with the evolving identity of the groups who considered the Bible sacred.

Keeping in mind that the formation of the Bible is tied to the history of evolving social groups, we must consider three lines of development that converge to form the recognition of the Bible as a sacred text.

The first line of convergence has to do with the gradual solidifying or fixing of the actual version or reading of the individual books that came to be considered sacred. Perhaps this issue is easiest to see in a contemporary setting. If you or I were to visit several different Christian churches on a given weekend, we would encounter a variety of Bibles being used. Some might use the King James Version. Undoubtedly there would be several churches using the New International Version. We might find a Revised Standard Version. In the Roman Catholic denomination we would come across the New American Standard. While all claim to be the same Bible, these different versions do in fact read quite differently—both in the individual books brought together to form the Bible and in the actual wording of those individual books contained in the Bible.

The same thing was going on when the Hebrew Bible was being brought together and can easily be seen within the books of the Old Testament (for example, the different renditions of the Ten Commandments). Some of the differences are in wording and seem to be pretty insignificant, but other differences between the versions are much more important. The sorting out of these differences and settling on one favored reading as the one reading to set in stone and recognize as the preferred reading was a process that came to a head (if ever at all) between the fourth and sixth centuries C.E.

The second line of convergence that will point us toward the formation of a set "canon," or body of sacred literature, has to do with the competition between religious groups. Sacred texts, in our case the Christian Old Testament and the Hebrew Bible, didn't develop apart from the group using those texts.[2] Again, perhaps a contemporary example might help. Consider the differences between the Bibles used by Mormons, Jehovah's Witnesses, Roman Catholics, Eastern Orthodox, and Protestant groups. All of these different groups claim to be Christian; yet all use different forms of the Bible. Again, the same thing was happening when the Old Testament was being formed. Different groups within Judaism and, a little later on, the Christians all claimed to come from the same religious stock. As one or more of these groups emerged as dominant over all the others, so too the sacred text used by those dominant groups emerged as the standard or canon by which the texts of all the others were evaluated.

Finally, as we try to identify when texts were recognized as authoritative, sacred, and part of a set canon, we need to recognize that there are differences between formal or official pronouncements and informal or popular practice. In other words, the official pronouncements coming from the leaders of the religious groups should not be confused with what is actually practiced by the people in the pews. And this too has a complicating influence. Most of what we know about the early history of the Bible comes from the official pronouncements of religious leaders. Sometimes those pronouncements *followed* what most people commonly practiced, and sometimes those pronouncements were *designed to shape* what most people practiced. So the official pronouncements by themselves cannot be considered sure evidence describing the actual state of affairs at the time those pronouncements were made.

The three converging lines of influence can be diagrammed as follows:

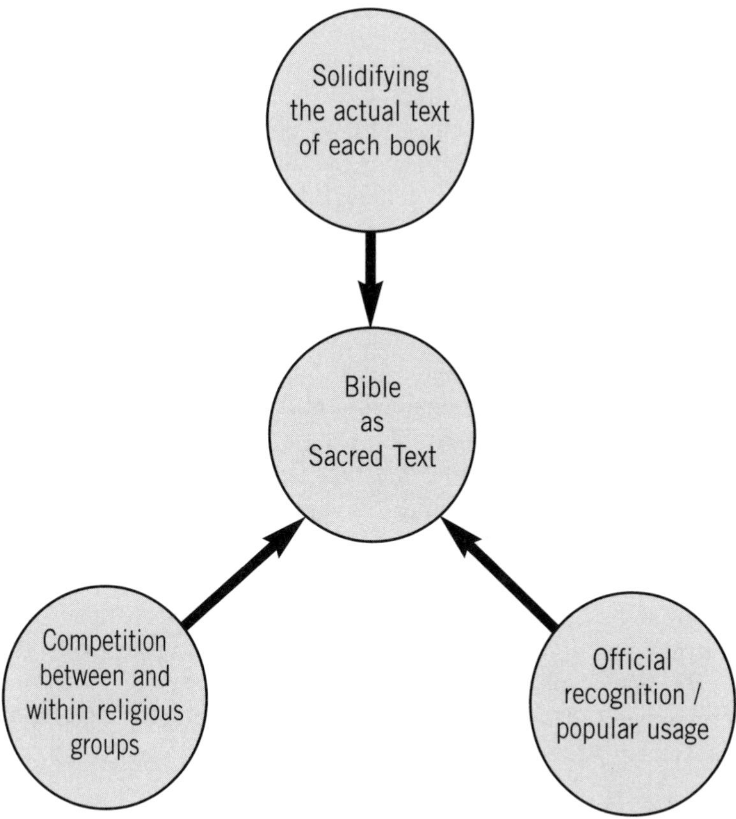

The point is: the development of a collection of sacred books (a canon) is a slow, messy, and gradual process. No matter how unsettling this may be to modern-day readers of the Bible, we can't get around the historical fact that sacred texts don't just happen overnight but are rather the result of lengthy processes that included debates, disagreements, and the struggle for power and dominance between different religious groups.

JUDAISM AND THE HEBREW BIBLE

Remembering the convergence of different lines from above and the way sacred texts are wrapped up in the lives of those groups using these texts, we should expect that major steps in the development of the sacred collection of books were matched by major social events in the lives of the people to whom the books belonged. For ancient Israel and developing Judaism, a series of significant events culminating in the mid-second century influenced the formation of the Hebrew Bible.

The social upheaval following the cataclysmic ending of the Bar Kochba Revolt of 135 C.E. gave a new sense of urgency to the Jewish people for the preservation of a sacred text. The Bar Kochba Revolt was a failed attempt to secure Jewish independence from the Romans, and when that revolt failed, Jerusalem was razed, the area was renamed, and it was made unlawful for Jews to inhabit the region. The temple, the sacrifices, and the symbolic center of religious life that the city of Jerusalem provided were now all gone, and this gaping vacuum gave rise to a new center—a sacred text—around which the Jewish community could reconstitute itself. Similar tragedies occurred earlier on for the Jewish community and its Israelite predecessors. The Babylonians' destruction of Jerusalem, the Maccabean Revolt, the Jewish Revolt, and finally the Bar Kochba Revolt all represented major social moments and upheavals calling into question the identity of the Jewish community.

Babylonian Destruction of Jerusalem (586 B.C.E.)	Maccabean Revolt (166–150 B.C.E.)	Jewish Revolt (70 C.E.)	Bar Kochba Revolt (135 C.E.)

In the midst of social upheaval a core identity was found in a collection of sacred books. The final push for solidifying the Hebrew Bible into an identifiable collection came in the form of a new religious group, the Christians, claiming to be related to Judaism but also circulating among themselves a whole new set of books.

There is good reason to think that the Hebrew Bible is the result of a four-step process of compilation.

- A core of text consisting of a form of Deuteronomy or parts of Deuteronomy began taking shape in the seventh century B.C.E. and traveled with the exiles from Jerusalem to Babylon in the early part of the sixth century B.C.E.

- As the exilic community began to return to Jerusalem and work started on reconstituting a new temple and rebuilding Jerusalem in the late sixth century and into the fifth century B.C.E., the "Deuteronomic" material from stage one was added to a mammoth body of historical tradition (much of Genesis through 2 Kings), telling the story of the reforming community and providing a sense of common history and identity.[3]
- About two centuries later (350–300 B.C.E.) a third body of material was added to the growing body of authoritative text—the prophetic collection extending from Isaiah to Malachi. This material, added to the Prophets, resulted in a subdivision of the Prophets into the Former Prophets (Joshua through 2 Kings) and the Later Prophets (Isaiah through Malachi).
- The impetus for the last section of the Hebrew Bible came first in the midst of the cultural and intellectual upheaval experienced in Jerusalem during a "Hellenistic Reform" that began in the second century B.C.E. and is evidenced in the turmoil leading to and following the Maccabean Revolt between 170 and 150 B.C.E. This process was renewed and extended even further by the chaos following the Jewish War of 70 C.E., in which the temple was destroyed and, by necessity, Judaism progressed toward becoming a decentralized religion. The Writings become firmly attached to the Torah and the Prophets during this three-century-long period of social change.

For some time, the developing Judaism owned a textual tradition that gave it a direction and identity; but in the first and second centuries C.E. it seemed important, in the face of severe threat by both war and religious competition, to formalize that textual tradition and, as it were, set it in stone. That textual tradition allowed a center for the community when Jerusalem and the religious rituals the city symbolized were gone. In addition, the textual tradition provided a marker, a distinguishing characteristic, separating Judaism from other religious groups—including the up-and-coming Christianity. This whole process seems to have been brought to a head and solidified into a widely recognized set of sacred books by the second or early third century C.E.

THE SETTLING OF THE WORDING OF THE SACRED BOOKS

Determining the list of which books to include in the Hebrew Bible and which books to exclude does not settle the matter. The actual wording of the books selected or recognized as sacred still needed to be worked out. There were different versions of the books that make up the Hebrew Bible being used by the religious faithful and it wasn't until the fifth through sixth centuries that one particular version emerged as the preferred reading, normative for most of Judaism.

A movement toward the standardization of how the books read was brought to a culmination in the fifth and sixth centuries by a group of people called the Masoretes. This remarkable academic and religious community left a significant legacy in the formation of the Hebrew Bible by standardizing the reading of the books that are included in the Hebrew Bible. In describing their own work, the Masoretes claim to have constructed a "fence around the Torah," protecting it from further additions and restraining it from further variations.[4] The Masoretes accomplished this standardization by providing notes, added to the text, and by inserting vowels into what was, before they did their work, a purely consonantal text. Perhaps it sounds strange to us in the West, but the Hebrew Bible, until the time of the Masoretes, was simply a long line of consonants strung together with very few punctuation marks or vowels to help in the reading of sentences or words! Could you imagine trying to read this page if all you saw was something like the following? *lttrsstrngtgthrwthnspcsprtngwrd-srvwlsrprdsrnythng* Not easy to read, especially if you aren't familiar with what the letters are supposed to say, or if you haven't heard them read out loud, or if you couldn't identify the story the string of letters is trying to tell. But this apparently nonsensical string of letters suddenly comes alive when the vowels are inserted (*letters strung together with no space separating words or vowels or periods or anything*). That's exactly what the oldest Hebrew Bibles were like. But it worked. People were familiar with what it was supposed to say; they did know the stories and so used the letters on the scrolls simply as aids or helps when memory faltered. Eventually, however, people lost that familiarity. To counter this loss of familiarity and the growing disagreement over what the words meant, the Masoretes standardized an interpretation of the Hebrew Bible by the addition of their helps. This standardized version of the Hebrew Bible came to be known as the Masoretic Text or MT for short. With the Masoretic Text we have a drive toward a standardized "set in stone" reading of the Hebrew Bible.

We can now suggest a rough timeline tracing major steps leading toward the development of the Hebrew Bible:

Compilation of the Deuteronomic Core	Compilation of the Epic History	Compilation of the Prophets	Compilation of the Writings	Tri-Part Division / List of Books In each Division	Masoretic Setting of the text
7th B.C.E.	5th B.C.E	4th B.C.E	1st–2nd C.E.	2nd–3rd C.E.	5th–6th C.E.

CHRISTIAN OLD TESTAMENT

With the introduction of the MT we have a convenient place to begin talking about the Christian Old Testament, for the Christian Old Testament is wrapped up in the differences between two versions of what became the Hebrew Bible: the Septuagint and the Masoretic Text. The history leading to the recognition of the Christian Old Testament is not a smooth and straight-line process of development and to some degree plays off the development of the Hebrew Bible for Judaism. The same three vectors we saw in the development of the Hebrew Bible (formal recognition and informal practice; competing religious groups; solidifying the actual reading of the books) are involved in the development of the Christian Old Testament.

Although there is substantial agreement between the Masoretic Text and the Septuagint (a pre-first-century Greek version of the Hebrew Bible tradition), there are also significant differences. Not only are there differences in the order, length, and wording of some of the books, but the way the two collections are structured is different as well. As can be seen from the chart below, the Septuagint (often referred to as the LXX) has a much different order of books than the order found in the Hebrew Bible.

Septuagint	Roman Catholic Old Testament	Protestant Old Testament
Pentateuch • Genesis • Exodus • Leviticus • Numbers • Deuteronomy **Historical Books** • Joshua • Judges • Ruth • Reigns (1 and 2 Samuel, 1 and 2 Kings) • Chronicles (1 and 2) • 1 Esdras • 2 Esdras (Ezra-Nehemiah) • Esther • Judith • Tobit • 1-4 Maccabees	**Pentateuch** • Genesis • Exodus • Leviticus • Numbers • Deuteronomy **Historical Books** • Joshua • Judges • Ruth • 1 Samuel • 2 Samuel • 1 Kings • 2 Kings • 1 Chronicles • 2 Chronicles • Ezra • Nehemiah • Tobit • Judith • Esther	**Pentateuch** • Genesis • Exodus • Leviticus • Numbers • Deuteronomy **Historical Books** • Joshua • Judges • Ruth • 1 Samuel • 2 Samuel • 1 Kings • 2 Kings • 1 Chronicles • 2 Chronicles • Ezra • Nehemiah • Esther

Poetical Books • Psalms • Proverbs • Canticles (Ecclesiastes) • Song of Songs (Song of Solomon) • Job • Wisdom of Solomon • Sirach • Psalms of Solomon **Prophetical Books** • Hosea • Amos • Micah • Joel • Obadiah • Jonah • Nahum • Habakkuk • Zephaniah • Haggai • Zechariah • Malachi • Jeremiah • Isaiah* • Baruch • Lamentations • Letter of Jeremiah • Ezekiel • Susanna • Daniel • Bel and the Dragon	• 1 Maccabees • 2 Maccabees **Wisdom Books** • Job • Psalms • Proverbs • Ecclesiastes • Song of Songs (Song of Solomon) • Wisdom • Sirach (Ecclesiasticus) **Prophetical Books** • Isaiah • Jeremiah • Lamentations • Baruch • Ezekiel • Daniel • Hosea • Joel • Amos • Obadiah • Jonah • Micah • Nahum • Habakkuk • Zephaniah • Haggai • Zechariah • Malachi	**Poetical Books** • Job • Psalms • Proverbs • Ecclesiastes • Song of Solomon **Prophetical Books** • Isaiah • Jeremiah • Lamentations • Ezekiel • Daniel • Hosea • Joel • Amos • Obadiah • Jonah • Micah • Nahum • Habakkuk • Zephaniah • Haggai • Zechariah • Malachi

* The books Jeremiah, Esther, and Daniel appearing in the LXX have material not found in their counterparts in the Masoretic Text. The Old Testament appearing in Roman Catholic versions of the Old Testament follows the LXX, whereas the Old Testament used by most Protestants follows the MT.

Generally, the order of books found in the Christian Old Testament follows the order of books found in the Septuagint. As for those books found in the Septuagint but not in the Hebrew Bible, they also account for some of the differences in the Bibles used today by Roman Catholics (who favor the Septuagint version) and Protestants (who adopted the Hebrew Bible [MT] of Judaism). Those books included in the Septuagint but not found in the Hebrew Bible are today called the Apocryphal books or the Deutero-Canonical books and are included in Bibles commonly used by the Roman Catholic denomination, but they are not included in the Bibles commonly used by Protestants. Various branches of the Eastern Orthodox Church also use the books that the Roman Catholic Church uses, but other additional minor variations exist among the branches of the Eastern Church.

WHY ARE THERE SO MANY DIFFERENT ENGLISH TRANSLATIONS?

The divergence among Old Testaments, some following the MT and some following the LXX, was given even greater support during the sixteenth century. One of the bedrock ideas driving the Protestant Reformation was the conviction that the Bible should be accessible to everyone. This led to a renewal of interest in the Old Testament and a motivation to translate the Old Testament into languages that people could understand. King James of England commissioned one of the most famous English translations in 1604, with a first edition appearing in 1611. This translation showed much greater respect for the Hebrew Bible (MT) than it did for the Septuagint and included only those books found in the Hebrew Bible. The animosity that existed in the sixteenth and seventeenth centuries between the Roman Catholic and Protestant branches of Christianity extended even to the preference of which version of the Old Testament was used by each. The Council of Trent (1545), a Roman Catholic council of church leaders called, in part at least, to deal with the Reformation problem, reaffirmed an acceptance of those books found in the Septuagint but not in the Hebrew Bible, calling them the "Deutero-Canonical" books (the "secondarily canonical" books). So with the Council of Trent and the publishing of the King James Bible (KJV), the Old Testament as we know it today was pretty much set. One version was printed for use among Roman Catholics and one version was printed for use among Protestants. In fact, the KJV was by far and away the best-selling English version of the Bible until the mid 1980s, when the New International Version (NIV) replaced it as the best-selling English version. Today, the trend toward separate versions of the Old Testament—one for Roman Catholics and one for Protestants—is moderating a bit. Some versions of the Bible, intended for use by many different denominations, include the "Apocryphal" (the Deutero-Canonical books) books in a section all their own, even though there are still versions that seek to maintain their religious separateness (most notably, the New American Version for Roman Catholics and the New International Version for Protestants).

THE FORMATION OF THE NEW TESTAMENT

For the earliest followers of Jesus, religious authority was found not in a book or in a collection of books but in a person. Jesus was the authority to which others appealed. In some of the earliest letters of Paul (an important leader and advocate of the early Christian movement), he refrains from seeking direction from the authority of a book but rather appeals directly to Jesus and secondarily to those who knew Jesus best.[5] In fact, an argument can be made that "if the earliest churches intended their successors to have a canon of scripture, either Old Testament or New Testament, we have no clear tradition to that effect."[6] It was only gradually, with the passage of time, that documents began to assume an air of authority within the community of Jesus followers.

In the first two centuries after Jesus there were a lot of Christian writings circulating among the followers of Jesus. So how was it that some of them found their way into this New Testament while others did not? The New Testament did not develop in one fell swoop; rather, it is the accumulation of smaller groupings of books combined together with other collections to form the whole New Testament.[7]

The formation of a sacred text, both Old Testament and New Testament, was not a process only about books but was also a story about an emerging church body, power structure, and a set of correct or orthodox beliefs. The movement toward a "canon" (an official set of authoritative writings) was part of a larger movement toward a monolithic faith within the Christian community. Competing forms of Christianity or variations in the way that people thought about Jesus either simply fell by the wayside or were pushed aside in favor of what would emerge as the "orthodox" position accompanied by a set of sacred texts that affirmed the correctness of the winning group.

Most believe that the New Testament grew in three stages with the formation of three smaller collections of New Testament writings.

- One of the earliest collections, if not the earliest, to be gathered together was a collection of writings by Paul (although Paul's actual authorship of some of these books is doubted). The earliest collection of Paul books, in the middle part of the second century, contained 1 and 2 Corinthians, Romans, Ephesians, 1 and 2 Thessalonians, Galatians, Philippians, Colossians, and Philemon.[8] Later, 1 and 2 Timothy and Titus were added, and finally Hebrews was included in the group, even though this book has features that make it quite distinct from the other "Paul" books (it may be that this collection is what the writer of 2 Peter 3:5 had in mind).
- The next grouping to emerge in this path toward the New Testament was a collection of Gospels. The

four, now appearing in the New Testament, were all written in the later part of the first century or the first part of the second century C.E. at the latest. But these four represent only a fraction of the Gospels that were written and used by the early groups of Jesus followers.[9] Some of these can be read even today and preserve fascinating stories and traditions about Jesus. Yet, among all these writings, four seemed to be most popular. Rather than including only one or two of these Gospels, or some sort of harmonization among the four, leaders of the early Christian church reached a political compromise and all four—each with its own perspective, bias, and unique story to tell—were retained and added to the collection bearing the name of Paul.

- It wasn't until the end of the second century (i.e., the third generation of Jesus followers) that the word *scripture* was used as a description for the growing collection of authoritative writings composed by and used by early followers of Jesus.[10] By the end of the second century, the Paul collection and the fourfold Gospel collection were fixed.[11] A third grouping of writings would take much longer to standardize. This last grouping of writings included letters such as 1 Peter and 1 John that were written to very general audiences and were accepted as part of the "New Testament" in the late second and early third centuries. Other writings—James, 2 Peter, 2 and 3 John, as well as Jude and Revelation—had a much harder time of it and their place in the canon was questioned far into the sixth century. As late as the Reformation in the sixteenth century, Luther had serious concerns about James and Revelation.

The three steps leading to the establishment of the New Testament collection can be diagrammed as below:

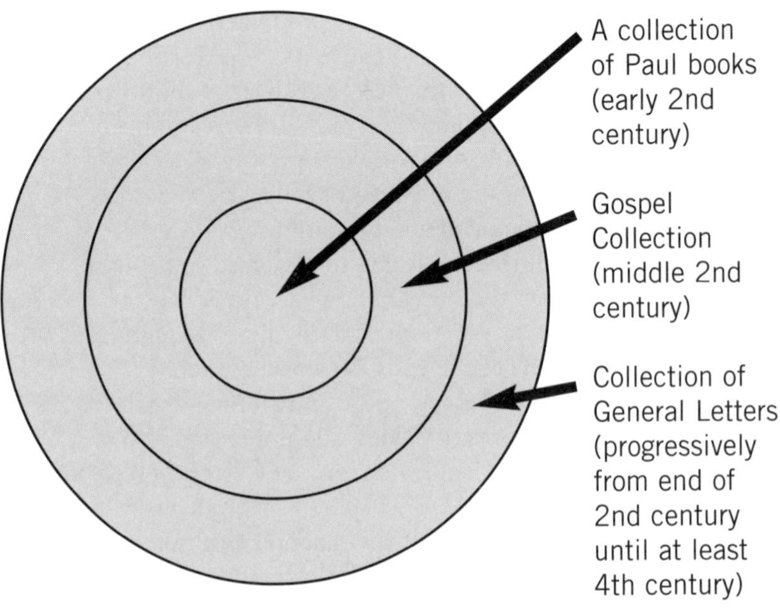

A series of church councils met in the late fourth century and from these councils various lists of New Testament books were produced. There was a fair amount of disagreement over which books to include even into the fourth century. As a general rule, books were considered for the New Testament that were: (1) thought to have been written by an apostle, (2) addressed to and used by the church at large, and (3) met some standard of orthodox belief (and this criterion may have been the most important in the long run).[12] These three criteria were applied only generally, as some of the books were certainly not authored by the person whose name the book bears and some were addressed to very specific audiences. The test of orthodoxy tends to be very circular and can be criticized as simply supporting the power position of those making the decision regarding the acceptability of a book. The drive toward uniformity of faith among the originally quite diverse Christian communities was accompanied by a drive toward a commonly recognized body of sacred texts that all the Christian communities could accept as authoritative.

GETTING BACK TO THE ORIGINAL TEXT

The list of books comprising the New Testament was pretty much settled by the sixth century (although books like Revelation had a much harder time of it),[13] but that's only part of the story. There are numerous very old copies of the New Testament books preserved in libraries and museums around the world. In addition, there are hundreds if not thousands of bits and pieces, fragments of papyrus that contain parts of old copies of the New Testament books. These bits and pieces don't all read the same. Every New Testament book that commonly appears in Bibles today is in fact an edited version presenting what scholars believe to be the best rendition culled from these old manuscripts, fragments, and pieces.

There is no ancient Greek manuscript that reads just like the New Testament we have today. Many find it initially disturbing, but the fact remains that the New Testaments commonly used today are translated from Greek versions that are edited copies, comparing and compiling many old copies of the books of the New Testament or pasting together hundreds of small fragments of manuscripts of those books. To be sure, extreme care has been taken to try to get it right, to present a readable New Testament that is faithful to what the original must have looked like, but there is room for disagreement and some of the variations between modern translations are a result of those scholarly disagreements.

The Gospel of Mark provides a convenient example of how this disagreement has worked its way into English translations. Some early copies of Mark end the Gospel at 16:8, whereas other copies extend chapter 16 all the way through verse 20. Various modern translations utilize different means in attempting to deal with this debate over how the Gospel should end. The New International Version places a line separating verse 8 from verse 9; the Revised Standard Version uses a space between lines; and the New American Version has an editorial note identifying verses 9 through 20 as "The Longer Version." The King James Version, however, makes no separation between verse 8 and verse 9, choosing to accept the Longer Version without comment. Examples like this one from Mark 16 could be repeated hundreds of times and are found in every book of the New Testament.

ENGLISH NEW TESTAMENTS

It can be maddening to pick up three different versions of the New Testament and find that all three offer different readings of any given passage. One of the main reasons for the difference in translations is the fact that our English New Testaments are based upon a compilation of fragments, bits and pieces of ancient manuscripts. Choosing the best reading, the reading thought to be closest to the original, isn't always easy. It isn't simply a matter of counting up which of the alternate readings has the most manuscripts or fragments supporting it, because not all the manuscripts and fragments are equally reliable. A judgment must be made and not all translation committees arrive at the same conclusion.

Some of the variation between modern translations is a result of choosing this or that variant reading for a given text. Additionally, some of the differences between modern language versions are a result of the difficulty inherent in trying to pick just the right wording to accurately convey what the translator believes to be the intent of the Greek text. And sometimes the differences in modern language translations are the result of the religious or theological biases of the translators creeping in and influencing the translation, leading to a conclusion of what the Greek text must mean, independent of any grammatical or manuscript evidence. The committees producing the best modern language translations work hard at minimizing bias and translator idiosyncrasy by subjecting each passage submitted by a translator to review, checks, and rechecks from other members of the committee. Despite the very best intentions and the most exacting translation possible, the fact remains, however, that our modern language New Testaments are approximate translations of edited Greek texts.

SO WHAT DOES ALL THIS MEAN FOR DOUBTERS?

The Bible didn't make its entrance into human history prepackaged and ready-made. Instead of falling into human history, the Bible came from within human history and was, during its formation, subject to the foibles and limitations of the people binding it together. So does this fact of history mean that the Bible is unreliable and therefore unable to communicate anything of lasting value? No, I don't think so. In fact, it may be that the Bible communicates more powerfully simply because it speaks to us as one of us. If we are to encounter the Bible as it really is, there are several important facts for us to keep in mind.

1. There never has been a "pure" original Bible now available for use that represents a direct line leading all the way back to the original author and the original writing. Instead, our modern language translations are the result of careful comparisons between ancient textual traditions and manuscript fragments that very closely approximate a hypothetical and ideal original. Each of the books now comprised in the Bible has been involved in a continuous and lively conversation with those who read it. That conversation has left its marks on the books. Most of those marks we can identify and evaluate as remnants of the Bible-reading conversation preceding our own reading. The point is that neither the books of the Bible nor we stand isolated but reside in a continuous, multigenerational stream. The books now making up the Bible have played an important part of that stream. The fact that the books of the Bible have undergone this rather convoluted history means they have never been put on a shelf, tucked out of the way and ignored and neglected, but have always, since their inception, drawn the attention of doubters like us.

2. The fact that the Bible developed slowly over time means that the Bible could never rest on its laurels. As the Bible was developing, each generation put it to the test to see what was useful and what was not. The books that we now have in the Bible have been put to the test and, for our predecessors at least,

were deemed valuable enough to pass on to generations following them. If we imagine the growth of the Bible as ripples spreading out from a stone thrown into a pond, we come close to imagining the lively and dynamic nature of the Bible. Those expanding ripples not only spread to include the second and third parts of the Hebrew Bible but also spread further to absorb a whole set of documents about Jesus and the implications of his life, death, and resurrection. Even though it doesn't appear that any more books will be added to the sacred canon anytime soon, those ripples still continue. In the process of reading and interpretation, the biblical texts still interact with those who read them and effect change no less now than when those texts were first written.

So let's get to the bottom line. What does all this mean for people like you and me who simply want to read the Bible and receive benefit from it? Does this remarkably complex history of translations, versions, and variations mean that God has been silenced and that the Bible is no longer a credible guide? Wouldn't it have been better if the Bible had simply fallen out of the sky or been written in the clouds for all to see? In short: no, probably not.

I've discovered that one of the remarkable things about the Bible is that this voice from within human history is able at the same time to call us out of our own moment in history and to speak to us of a reality beyond what we are able to see with our eyes. We have before us in the Bible a set of books, the Old and New Testaments, that have been processed through the crucible of real human experience—tried and tested, stretched and shaped, just like every one of us. We need to read the Bible mindful of its participation in this stream of history.

Perhaps an example from the Bible itself will help make clear what I'm trying to say. First Corinthians 15 includes one of the most inspiring and timeless passages in the whole Bible. Paul, the probable writer of this chapter, sets before us a vision of redemption that not even the grave can frustrate. None of us need be overwhelmed by the specter of death for, as he puts it, "Death is swallowed up in victory" (1 Corinthians 15:54) through a promised resurrection, made sure by the resurrection of Jesus. To support his celebration, Paul reaches far back in time, enlisting the help of two Old Testament prophets, Isaiah (25:8) and Hosea (13:14).

> O death, where is thy victory?
> O death, where is thy sting?

But in reaching back into the prophetic literature, Paul does not ask his readers to step out of the stream of history and return to the time of the prophets. Paul gives the prophetic passages a twist, for times have changed. What Isaiah holds out as a promise only for the Israelites and what Hosea asks only sarcastically, Paul exuberantly places into the grasp of all people everywhere! Everyone can now share the promise of a resurrection and life everlasting because the stream of history has now included the life, death, and resurrection of Jesus in its flow. From Paul's point of view, the Bible (the prophets Isaiah and Hosea) must be understood *within* the flow of history and not simply dropped into the flow of history. But the stream continues to flow. Just as Paul took us beyond the prophets Isaiah and Hosea, we too cannot ignore that Paul's time in history is not our own. Women don't need to be silent in church as Paul admonished just a few short verses earlier (1 Corinthians 14:34), for times have changed and the first-century Roman world is not our own.

Only the most obstinate and proud can escape the steady and sure march of time without bearing within them the marks of change and growth. In this regard, bearing in it the marks of time and history, the Bible speaks to us as living among us. If we eventually come to conclude that somehow or other God meets us in the Bible, this twisting, turning, and sometimes suspicious history of the Bible's origin means that God is ready to meet us and speak to us in the midst of the real stuff of life. The process of living leaves marks on us all—even on the Bible—and it may be that it is because of the struggle and the turmoil, as well as the joy and the peace, of real life that the words of the Bible speak with power.

CHAPTER FOUR

IS THE BIBLE SPIN FOR THE POWERFUL?

This may be the most important chapter in this entire book. In the last several chapters we saw how the Bible is all too frequently subject to the agenda and influence of people wishing to use it for their own purposes. The opening of the twenty-first century has witnessed the emergence of religious power on a global scale not seen since the sixteenth century. In this religious struggle for influence a good case can be made to conclude that the Bible has become a pawn, providing spin to validate the cause of those seeking power.

Individually and collectively, for good and for ill, all of us have been touched by religious power. There can be no doubt that religious fervor has had destabilizing and sometimes devastating effects at the beginning of the twenty-first century. Monks in Myanmar and Tibet carry the banner of social change. Religious sects in Texas, California, and Utah find themselves going toe-to-toe with legal and political adversaries. The phrase *radical Islamist terrorist* has become common fare, repeated incessantly and indiscriminately in newscast after newscast. In the United States, the line separating religious power and political power seems to have evaporated, at least during the campaign season.

For me, the label "Christian Warrior" represents a particularly troubling example of religious power. The label has been adopted by a whole host of organizations ranging from youth movements (including the *Jesus Camp* phenomenon), antigay legal groups, and patriotic and militaristic rallies. It also is used as a draw for online children's video games (www.kidwarriors.com). You can even buy the Full Armor of God Playset with which parents can be sure their "kids will be dressed for spiritual success when they put on this safe plastic costume" that, in the advertisement at least, looks for all the world like a crusader warrior's dress.[1] The array of websites including the "Christian Warrior" label is astonishing. One included the heading "Good News" in large, bold print above a photograph of a mosque that had just been bombed and destroyed (www.cwgn.us [9/26/07]). In some corners at least, the Christian gospel of peace is fast losing its way.

In the twenty-first century, religion has become a line drawn in the sand, used to divide and define opposing social groups. Caught up square in the middle of this power struggle is the Bible. Just like other religious texts, the Bible too has become a pawn in the power struggles that seem to characterize religious commitment. In this chapter, we will examine the way the Bible has become spin in the quest for power. It's an issue that doubters and nondoubters alike need to confront, for we are all caught in its dangerous web.

SEPARATE BUT EQUAL SWIMMING HOLES

I think we can all agree that the Bible has had for centuries a prominent place in Western culture. There can be no doubt that the Bible is a powerful book. There are, however, numerous reasons to question and to doubt the integrity and authenticity of the kind of power that has aggregated around the Bible. The Bible has been cited as the power and authority to champion all sorts of causes. Perhaps an example, removed a step or two historically, will give us a measure of objectivity.

John R. Rice, a firebrand preacher and a prolific author in the middle part of the twentieth century, ran a newsletter titled *The Sword of the Lord*. In his publication, Rice likened the Bible to a sword (interestingly the first weapon appearing in the Bible—in

Genesis 3:24—and sometimes used as a metaphor to describe the word of God) ready to strike down enemies on every side. The problem with swords, however, is they are only extensions, for better or for worse, of the person whose fingers grasp the handle. Writing in the mid-1960s, Rice felt inclined to comment on the racial tensions sweeping across America in that turbulent time. He claimed that his own opposition to racial integration was in fact "biblical" and used his "biblical" foundation to argue against racial intermarriage and for a degree of segregation that extended all the way to racially segregated swimming pools.[2]

Thankfully, times have changed, and, on this issue at least, Rice could now find very few willing to confirm his description of a "biblical" position. Yet, for doubters like me, Rice presents a very real challenge—in part because there are so many like him, using the Bible in the very same way, as spin, to promote their own preferences and agenda. Rice and the many like him force these questions: Is this all there is? Is the power of the Bible like a megaphone, simply amplifying the voice of the one waving it about? Does the Bible only shout the mantra of the day? Or does the Bible have a voice of its own, one that can speak to us, not just for us?

Doubters take this confusion of power very seriously, and even though John R. Rice is no longer with us, television and radio airwaves as well as Internet websites have become jam-packed with many others who are more than willing to take up the mantel of warrior, wielding the biblical sword.

AUTHORITY IN NAMING THE SACRED: JUST WHO *IS* IN CHARGE?

The matter of the Bible's authority is somewhat circular in nature. Believers claim that the Bible has authority. But all too often it's the authority of the person or group proclaiming the Bible's authority that gives the claim legitimacy—and so the circularity of the statement. In pronouncing the Bible sacred, an implicit claim is made that those voicing the pronouncement have the authority to do so. The Bible is "sacred" because somebody in authority said it's sacred. They have authority over the Bible. They claim to have the ability, and are exercising the right, to determine what is sacred and what is not. An argument can be made that it is the authority of the person, group, or institution calling the Bible sacred that allows the Bible to become authoritative.

Statements of the Bible's authority are really statements of the *relationship* between a person, group, or institution and the Bible. That relationship can be healthy, describing and resulting in positive benefits, or the relationship between the Bible and person, group, or institution can be unhealthy, characterized by a self-aggrandizing piety that is condemnatory of others. The point is that simply voicing the authority of the Bible is no guarantee of actually experiencing the Bible's authority. Often those shouting the Bible's authority the loudest are those very people most tempted to simply use the Bible as a proxy for their own ambition of authority and influence. The most blatant example of this I've ever seen is the frequent use of 1 Samuel 26:9 (do not put your hand against the "LORD's anointed") by a religious leader who is trying to deflect accusation for wrongdoing or attempting to win popular support for his or her own priorities and agenda. In this instance, the Bible's authority is called upon to affirm the authority or rightness of the person. Here, the Bible is simply a surrogate and aid for the authority of the individual.

In all cases, the relationship between people proclaiming the authority of the Bible and the Bible itself is a living relationship that is dynamic and changing—if you will, circular. This circularity in claiming the Bible's authority means that every generation must ask afresh the nature of the authority of the Bible and frame that authority in ways that are meaningful for the here and now.

AUTHORITY AND THE VERDICT OF EVIDENCE, MORE EVIDENCE, AND MUCH MORE EVIDENCE

For our generation the nature of the Bible's authority in relationship to various groups and institutions has been more than a little troublesome and, for many, is in crises. In the last part of the twentieth century and moving into the twenty-first century, the conversation on the authority of the Bible has been dominated by the imposition of definitions of knowledge—ways of looking at the world around us—that are foreign to the Bible itself. That is, in the twentieth century, judgments about the authority of the Bible were largely based on the perceived scientific accuracy of statements in the Bible or the completeness and correctness of the Bible's historical reporting. The premise is that accuracy of the Bible's descriptions proved the Bible's authority. Perhaps the best-known example of this endeavor is the attempt made by Josh McDowell to amass "*evidence that demands a verdict*" and "*more evidence that demands a verdict*."[3] In his publications, McDowell sought to prove the Bible's authority by showing its historical and scientific accuracy despite the fact that these scientific and historical characteristics, common to us, are quite different from the characteristics used by the biblical writers to describe their own understanding of life.[4]

We, at the beginning of the twenty-first century, are almost obsessed with matters such as archaeological confirmation of events, or the physics of a worldwide flood, or a staunch depiction of a six-day creationism. Some have used that preoccupation as a filter to claim that the Bible is authoritative. Based on the acceptance of what they consider to be its detailed and accurate renditions of historical events, as well as the Bible's ability to describe the biological, physical, and even cosmic characteristics of the universe, the Bible is deemed authoritative. A clear example of this kind of reasoning appeared in the "Faith Reflections" editorial column of our local newspaper. The writer was attempting to argue for the credibility of belief in God and an eternal life. In so doing, he wrote:

> I have found that I can count on the credibility of the God of the Bible because I can count on the credibility of the Bible. Whether it is the archaeological findings, unchanging scientific and medical concepts, or historical record, these have all confirmed the biblical record, as well as its credibility, above all

> other religious texts. Because of the archaeological, historical and scientific credibility of the Bible, I can trust it.[5]

The logical path utilized by this writer is fairly common. That logical path involves two steps:

- I can count on God because I can count on the Bible.
- I can count on the Bible because I can amass historical and scientific evidence to prove the accuracy of its statements.

Notice what happens when this foundation—relying on historical confirmation and archaeological and scientific poof—begins to crack and crumble. When the sword cuts the other way, when history and science offer evidence to call into question scientifically and historically interpreted statements in the Bible, the Bible and then God are cast into doubt. This has happened many times. Imprudent and overly ambitious claims to archaeological, historical, and scientific proof have caused this house of cards to fall. For, using the same lens of science and history, others have concluded the Bible faulty, primitive, legendary, or just plain wrong in its understanding of historical events and cosmic reality, and so are unable to concede any authority to the writings. When using the lens of archaeology, science, or history to either prove or disprove the Bible, you usually find what you're looking for. The truth of the matter is that the Bible simply won't fit into that box.

The failure of the debate using categories of science and history has resulted in a crisis that has seriously diminished the recognized authority of the Bible.[6] Using the argument of science and history, many have intentionally or unintentionally attempted to use the authority of the Bible to legitimize their own authority. As many of the people using the science and history argument have become increasingly irrelevant, so too has the Bible.

The attempt to force the Bible into the box of science and history is only one example of a larger and more pervasive problem.

Attempts to make the Bible speak with a voice dominated by science or history amount to attempts to wield power over the Bible, to mold the Bible into our own image. Power over the Bible has been attempted in other ways as well and we do well to think about them.

POWER *OVER* THE BIBLE

In the example I used at the beginning of this chapter, Rice attempted to change the beliefs and actions of his readers (segregating swimming pools) based on the authority of the Bible. In so doing, Rice exercised authority over the Bible. This power-authority relationship has been attempted numerous times and represents a power *over* the Bible. This power *over* the Bible is the kind of power now most visible in the U.S. public arena. It is a power that creates hype and sensation. It is the power attempted when enlisting the Bible to provide commentary on the September 11 tragedy as an occasion to advance a social agenda against the ACLU, against a particular sexual orientation, and against particular abortion rights policies. It's the power—presented as the key to unlock the wealth of heaven—that television evangelists promise when pleading for money from viewing audiences. It is the power attempted by others seeking to persuade voters to vote for political candidates who are on God's side. It is the power forming young children who assume the "God's Warrior" persona as they combat dangerous enemies while playing video games. This form of power is expressed when persons, institutions, or groups make pronouncements about the Bible or use the Bible to validate their own position or prestige.

Sometimes power over the Bible can express itself quite innocently and unintentionally. If you've read the Bible much at all, you will eventually begin to wonder: What does the Bible say about this or that problem or issue facing us today? It's a good question asked by honest people intent on finding moral guidance through life's complex problems. Unfortunately, what can occasionally happen is that our question seeks an unambiguous answer when sometimes the Bible answers in more than one voice—challenging us to live with the ambiguity, to do our best in making just and good decisions without guarantees, to live by faith. If the ambiguity becomes intolerable, the reader simply emphasizes one biblical voice over all others, proclaiming it to be the best (and sometimes only) resolution or advice applied to the current situation. A "Bible within a Bible" is constructed that allows one text to speak with more authority than the others. Usually the "Bible within the Bible" will be the Gospels (and often the words in red letters—the quotations of Jesus) or some of the smaller books near the end of the New Testament. The problem with this approach is that it is all too easy for the "Bible within the Bible" to be simply a reflection of the interpreter's own preferences and not an accurate expression of the multiple voices speaking to us from the pages of the biblical text. If the "Bible within the Bible" is granted special or elevated authority, an effective authority over the Bible has been achieved.

Certainly, ours is not the first generation confronting this challenge of using religious authority to inappropriately wield power over others. The writer of 1 Peter 5:3 addresses the same issue that we've been considering. In this verse, spiritual leaders are challenged to care for others "not as domineering over those in your charge but being examples to the flock." In other words, the power (presumably based upon a sacred text tradition or similar expertise) to influence others is best conveyed not in a commanding fashion but as a role model. The leader has experienced the transforming power of the sacred text and simply lets that transformation live out in front of others. The power referenced in 1 Peter is evidenced not in authoritative commands but by testimony, by the witness that says to others: Come and see!

POWER *OF* THE BIBLE

The exercise of power *over* the Bible amounts to an attempt to make the Bible fit. It's an attempt to make the Bible conform to the user's own outlook on life and to use the Bible as evidence supporting his or her own preferences. But there is another kind of power at work with the Bible as well. The other kind of power at play in the Bible is not a power *over* the Bible, a power that can be controlled and molded to private agendas. For, as has been evidenced time and again, the Bible is resilient. The Bible has resisted this use of power and instead the power *of* the Bible has reasserted itself.

Before we continue, I need to pause a moment. I now find myself in a dilemma. If the power of the Bible is authentic and real, the best I can do is attempt to describe that power as I've encountered it and observed it in others. Yet my description could easily become an attempt to impose my agenda on you and could amount to a power over the Bible. I don't want to do that. I am mindful that as you read this book we are journeying together, airing our questions, and testing our answers. As you read the next several paragraphs, consider what you read, but please do not accept my observations or conclusions without putting them to the test for yourself. If there really is a power of the Bible, it should be available for you to experience no less than for me.

The most unnerving thing about the power of the Bible, in my experience, is that this power has been unexpected and uncontrollable. It has changed me in ways I neither expected nor really wanted. I've found that the best descriptions of the power of the Bible are only partial and tend to express how the Bible has been *formative* for an individual rather than *normative* for a group. Normative power tends to be power over the Bible, in which persons or groups attempt to make their own perceptions of the Bible normative for everyone. Normative power is an imposition from the outside. Formative power is a power at work to change us from the inside out. It is this kind of power (from the inside out) that is most described in the pages of the Bible itself. The power of the Bible is often described in the Bible as the *word of God*. We'll consider the *word of God* phrase at a later point. For now, it's enough that the word of God, at least as it is described in the Bible itself, is a moment of change. When applied to the Bible, the word of God amounts to the power of the Bible over the reader.[7]

THE TRANSFORMATIVE POWER OF THE BIBLE: A DIFFERENT KIND OF SPIN

The power of the Bible amounts to a different kind of spin that has the ability to transform the reader. In my opinion, this is the most authentic form of religious power and is the power at the core of the expressed agenda or spin of the Bible writers themselves. John 20:30-31 provides a clear example. "Now Jesus did many other signs in the presence of the disciples, which are not written in this book; but these are written that you may believe that Jesus is the Christ, the Son of God, and that believing you may have life in his name." We could look at many other examples, all demonstrating that each and every biblical book has its own agenda or spin.[8] The writers of the Bible experienced something they thought to be life changing and of benefit to others within their own spheres of influence. They wrote to convince others of those benefits. Taken as a whole, the agenda, spin, and power of the Bible is seen most dramatically in its ability to pull the reader into a reality greater than that which we see with our eyes.[9]

The power of the Bible has been transformative for me. This power is most evident not in dispassionate discussions about the Bible but in the experience of the Bible.[10] The power of the Bible, at least as I've experienced it, has at times offered comfort beyond my wildest dreams. But the power of the Bible has also dogged me incessantly. It has broken me and forced me to change attitudes and values I once held dearly. The power of the Bible has demonstrated to me the limits of my own control and has subjected me to forces and ambitions much bigger than myself. In my experience, this power of the Bible will not be harnessed and shows up at the most unexpected of times. The power of the Bible tends to be more personal and rarely shouts.

As near as I can tell, the transformative power of the Bible draws us into a different reality—the kingdom of God—and in so doing encourages us to redefine ourselves as well as everything around us. It begins with a self-redefinition.[11] The reader of the

Bible is confronted with a vision of self, primarily characterized as *created, loved,* and *forgiven* by God. A deep current running through the whole of the biblical text is a way of defining the human experience as created by God, loved by God, and forgiven by God. We are encouraged not to define ourselves as teacher, electrician, homemaker, or student. Neither are we encouraged to see ourselves primarily as husband, wife, child, or parent. Above all these, we are encouraged to see ourselves created by God in order to be loved by God and forgiven by God. This great trilogy of self-identification begins in the opening chapters of the Bible and is the real point of the creation story in Genesis. From there the reader is led on a mighty panoramic sweep through the pages of the Old Testament where, over and over again, the Creator acts to call back and make all of creation whole. In the words of Isaiah:

> For thus says the LORD,
> who created the heavens. . . .
> "Turn to me and be saved,
> all the ends of the earth!" (Isaiah 45:18-22)

The same theme is carried on in the New Testament. After having established that all the universe is the work of the Creator, John moves from his introduction to that very powerful and comprehensive statement: "For God so loved the world that he gave his only Son, that whoever believes in him should not perish but have eternal life" (John 3:16). When Paul, another author of books in the New Testament, considers our status as a "new creation" in Christ (Romans 8; 2 Corinthians 5:16-19; Ephesians 2:8-20), he is caught up in wonder of what it means to be created, loved, and forgiven by God. The New Testament ends in a massive starburst in which this triad of created, loved, and forgiven envelops the whole cosmos, resulting in a new heaven and earth in which there is no place for death, crying, or pain (Revelation 21:1-4). Created, loved, and forgiven—not sometime off in the future, but right now—are the primary lenses through which we see all our other roles and places in life. The power of the Bible is in providing us a lens by which to better see a world in which each of us is created, loved, and forgiven. This is the transforming power of the Bible.

But here's the thing. This kind of power is unpredictable. It requires a meeting between the reader and the Bible that is never quite the same for any two of us. The books of the Bible give us tools with which to make sense out of life. These tools become most powerful when put to the test—when applied by the reader. Since no two of us live life exactly the same, the powerful application of the books is never just the same.

The power and authority of the Bible are best evident not in arguments about the Bible but in the transformation of its readers. When through the Bible this transforming power is unleashed, it tends to redefine those who come under its influence. Created by God, loved by God, and forgiven by God become defining characteristics that transform the reader in a manner consistent with the way we are seen by God. Consequently, when attempting to evaluate the integrity of religious power and authority—even of the Bible—the best test remains: by their fruits you will know them.

CHAPTER FIVE

WHY IS THE BIBLE SO VIOLENT?

The most detestable wickedness, the most horrid cruelties, and the greatest miseries that have afflicted the human race have had their origin in this thing called revelation, or revealed religion. . . . Whence arose all the horrid assassinations of whole nations of men, women and infants, with which the Bible is filled, and the bloody persecutions and tortures unto death, and religious wars, that since that time have laid Europe in blood and ashes—whence arose they but from this impious thing called revealed religion? . . . What is it that we have learned from this pretended thing called revealed religion? Nothing that is useful to man, and everything that is dishonorable to his Maker. What is it the Bible teaches us?—rapine, cruelty, and murder.[1]

—*Thomas Paine*

Although I suspect most of us would not express ourselves as forcefully as Thomas Paine, many of us can resonate with his objection. The Bible is a violent book. There's no getting around it and there is no use trying. In an age that has witnessed an increase in religiously sponsored violence, sobering questions are being asked about the role of the Bible in forming religious values and attitudes. For doubters this is a serious issue but not a new one. In fact, at least one writer of the biblical text struggled with the same question and inserted his own moral resolution to the apparent atrocity of the genocide among Canaanite nations during the Israelite conquest of Palestine (Genesis 15:13-16). A man named Marcion in the second century and Thomas Jefferson of the eighteenth century both struggled with the brutality found in the pages of the Bible and resolved the dilemma by simply ripping out those offending passages. Yet for most of us the fact of violence and brutality in the Bible remains, and once again the presence of this dark side has forced us to reconsider the validity of the message the Bible has to offer.

HELL ON EARTH

The problem of the Bible's violence was shoved square in my face some years back. A while ago I spent some time in eastern Africa. The region had been devastated by both famine and war, and the human toll was staggering. It was a violent place and a violent time. In my journeys, I happened to meet a medical professional who was doing the best she could to alleviate suffering at one of the many refugee camps that had sprung up in the area. Patti (not her real name) knew what violence was—she stared it down every day and was dedicated to doing all she could to help its victims. She considered her work a service to God. I think Patti was right. She was a servant of God. Sometimes at day's end the incessant demands would take their toll and she would talk to the rest of us about what she had experienced. I remember thinking, at the time, that her descriptions were a therapy of sorts. She was debriefing, trying to make sense of the suffering and pain by telling us about it and thereby allowing us into her world, moderating her own sense of loneliness and isolation. She talked about the broken bodies, the emaciated children, the loneliness, fear, and overwhelming sadness that followed in the wake of war and drought. Mothers in deep agony over wasting children, with no means of help, and children alone and lost without parent or friend were frequent parts of Patti's descriptions. Those camps were hell on earth, and the worst part is that none of it was exaggerated.

During one of those evening conversations, it happened to come out that I had an interest in the Old Testament and even taught it at the college level for a living. Although it's been quite a number of years now, I can still remember Patti's reaction as if it were only yesterday. As I described my background and love for the Old Testament, Patti froze, staring at me in disbelief—and then she erupted! "How can anybody spend their life studying that stuff? I've never read a more violent book in my life—and to think that God is going around killing people all the time or ordering others to do his dirty work for him!" These words that I've just recited are accurate. They are what Patti said. But they do not do justice to the emotion of that moment. Patti was angry and devastated all at once. Not angry with me but angry with God—or at least the God that she read about in the Bible. You see, she knew firsthand the horror that violence can produce.

We read in Joshua 10:30 that "the LORD gave it [Libnah] also and its king into the hand of Israel; and he struck it with the edge of the sword, and every person in it; he left no one remaining in it" (NRSV). Verses like this one could be repeated literally dozens of times—not to mention a description of a divinely sponsored flood that kills all humanity except one family (Genesis 6:7), or the destruction of whole nations (Joshua 10:14; 11:20) and the exile of peoples throughout the Near East (Amos 9:7-8), reaching to a level of infanticide and war crimes that would make any of us shudder (Hosea 13:16). Most of us tend to read these descriptions quite quickly and in a detached fashion. But Patti knew firsthand the smell of an infected wound, the agony associated with a severed limb, and the pain of an unavoidable but tragically slow death. Patti saw young children weeping over the loss of and separation from a parent, and missing everything that gives life order: a meal, a place to stay, and a comforting hug. Patti heard their cries. And you need to know: the echoes of those cries last a long, long time.

But none of us is exempt. All of Patti's experience is right there—right before us in those words: "and he struck it with the edge of the sword." When you let yourself think about the meaning of those words, they do begin to become quite repulsive. Those simple words represent horrors that no one should be forced to endure. For Patti violence and the hell it creates were unacceptable. And to read about divinely sponsored violence in the Bible made, for her, the Bible unacceptable as well. Patti's objection was a real one. None of us should shrink from expressing our revulsion over the violence we read about in the Bible. And like it or not, we need to think about it.

If you choose to tackle this problem, let me offer a word of caution. Some problems are phantoms that fade away the more that you think about them. They are only problems because our information is wrong or because our own nervousness and anxieties create mountains out of molehills. This one is not like that at all. In fact, this problem gets bigger and more serious the more you mull it over. Patti was right on target and it's high time for an accounting. So let's give it a go.

THE BIBLE IS NO FAIRY TALE

One of the enduring qualities that commends the Bible to each generation is its ability to capture and describe the human condition. In many ways, reading the Bible is like looking in a mirror. We can see an awful lot about ourselves in its pages. Like it or not, violence is part of our shared reality, having touched every one of us. If the Bible had no descriptions of violence, no pain and no suffering in its depiction of the human condition, it would be a fairy tale. Above all else, the Bible is not a fairy tale. So the real problem is not that violence is in the Bible. Rather, the problem is: why is violence so much a part of the human condition and why does God seem to rely on violent means? The Bible just aggravates things by providing descriptions of violence that make God complicit, if not the main culprit, in a seemingly unending litany of tragedy. Isn't there a better way to run a universe? Or is the God of the Bible simply not bothered by the suffering violence causes? Or worse still, does God in some perverse way enjoy our suffering? Is God an abusive father? Or failing this line of questioning, is the Bible plain wrong? Are its violent descriptions of God either woefully out-of-date or simply reflections of violent people seeking to make God over in their own image? These seem to me to be the real concerns when levelheaded people, people like Patti, object to the descriptions of violence contained in the pages of the Bible.

IS THE BIBLE OUT-OF-DATE?

Let's try solving this problem by peeling it back one layer at a time, like peeling an onion, in order to see if we can get to the very heart of the matter. First, let's begin by asking if the Bible is simply out-of-date. Were those violent descriptions of God and God's actions simply a reflection of the time in which the pages were first written? Perhaps they did describe how people thought God acted way back then, but now it simply won't work.

To be sure, every page of the Bible is conditioned by the place and time in which it was written. If the Bible, or any book, is to be taken seriously, we need to read it on its own terms. So, while it doesn't excuse the violence, it does at least make it a bit more understandable if we remember that parts of the Bible story (some of the early parts of the Old Testament) are the nationalistic accounts of a people trying to make their way in the midst of a hostile world. Just as every nation claims God as a partner every time hostilities break out, ancient Israel did the same. The remarkable thing about the Bible is that this portrait of a national God, fighting unmercifully on behalf of a small and fledgling nation, gives way to a majestic view of a God who claims all people as special and precious.

This is where the Bible's participation in the stream of history, seen in chapter 2, is important to remember. The Bible is an anthology of many books, each with its own plan, theme, and distinct message or contribution to the whole collection. Some of these books, particularly in the Old Testament, have been edited together into a lengthy epic story recounting the formation, history, and demise of the ancient Israelite state.[2] As the story moves along, a plot develops, circumstances evolve, and, just like in any story, the early part of the story cannot be simply lifted out and reinserted into the last part of the story without consideration of all that has transpired in between. The Bible is not a flat snapshot, like a newspaper article; it is more like a movie, with development and drama that unfolds.

This is not to say that the end of the Bible makes the beginning obsolete or unnecessary. Not at all. As the story told by the Bible moves along, each episode builds upon the previous. In this regard, the Bible truly is remarkable. Later biblical writers pull forward into the present the earlier ideas, descriptions, and events, with new meanings and applications attached to those "pulled forward" passages. In chapter 2 we saw how the writer of Matthew pulled parts of the earlier Old Testament into the present through his "fulfillment" descriptions of Jesus. The writer of Hebrews pulled earlier parts of the Bible into the present by finding in those earlier portions information about Jesus.

The same happens within the various parts of the Old Testament itself. Early in the story of the Israelite nation, God is depicted as a national deity with particular concern and passionate care expressed for the fledging Israelite nation. Israel's God devastates the Egyptian nation (Exodus 7–13), destroys a pursuing Egyptian army (Exodus 14), and annihilates several small nations (Numbers 31; 33:51-52) who happen to occupy land promised to Israel by their God. This early part of the story makes very clear that God will go to extreme lengths to care and provide for God's people. In return, the "people of God" are taught that their own well-being is conditioned by adherence to a moral way of life summarized in love for God (Deuteronomy 6:4) and neighbor (Leviticus 19:18). As the Old Testament story progresses, however, the nationalistic concerns of the one Israelite group of people, so clearly expressed early on, become overshadowed by a perception of the Divine's compassion for all people everywhere. Even Israel's archenemies, Assyria and Egypt, are looked on with divine favor, and the nationalistic pride of Israel is replaced by a vision of a new social order in which all people experience peace and safety. "On that day Israel will be the third with Egypt and Assyria, a blessing in the midst of the earth, whom the LORD of hosts has blessed, saying 'Blessed be Egypt my people, and Assyria the work of my hands, and Israel my heritage'" (Isaiah 19:24-25 NRSV).

The passionate care God directed to Israel—care that was seen early in the story—is pulled forward and now applied to all people everywhere. Just as a plot is developed in a novel or a movie, where the earlier situations provide the backdrop for the last chapter or final scene, it's the nationalistic and warring backdrop seen early in the biblical story that makes these more universal claims, seen later in the biblical story, so astounding! The first part of the biblical story sets us up for a truly amazing finish.

This notion of pulling forward is seen quite clearly in another part of the Bible, with direct bearing on our question of violence in the Bible. Matthew 5–7 contains one of the most amazing pieces of literature that I know. It's called the Sermon on the Mount and represents the teaching of Jesus boiled down and presented in a very dense and hard-hitting speech or sermon. In the early part of the sermon Jesus presents a series of ethical norms, using as a backdrop statements either from the Hebrew Bible or moral norms based on the Hebrew Bible tradition (Matthew 5:21-48). He introduces each moral precept with the phrase "You have heard it said" and then quotes a passage from the Hebrew Bible or the moral tradition springing from the Hebrew Bible (Matthew 5:21, 27, 31, 33, 38, 43). The amazing part comes next. After quoting the older tradition—the "you have heard that it was said"—he goes on to say, "But I say to you" (Matthew 5:22, 28, 32, 34, 39, 44), followed by an ethical norm that pulls forward the old moral statement. Invariably, the new morality pronounced by Jesus is a movement away from violence. In other words, Jesus envisioned a human society in which the old moral norms, each written to make sense in a specific time and place, could now be refashioned to reflect the new circumstances of a different time and place. The old norms could not simply be recited and applied verbatim (tearing them out of the early part of the story and plopping them down in the later part), but rather were pulled forward and made applicable in the here and now by molding them to the new circumstances and realities in the present—circumstances that included the presence of the kingdom of God now available to Jew and Gentile, slave and free, male and female.

This is not to say there was anything inherently wrong with those old moral norms. Take for example the "eye for an eye and a tooth for a tooth" law of retribution referred to in Matthew 5:38. When this idea first made its way into the biblical record (Exodus 21:23-24 and Leviticus 24:19-20), it was intended as a very practical legal principle to limit the punishment that could be levied against the offender by making the punishment fit the crime. The principle was intended for implementation in a specific social setting at a specific time and place. The moral norm protected the offender from a punishment far worse than the crime. The law was amazingly egalitarian, not allowing the socially or legally powerful unlimited legal sway over the less powerful—even if the less powerful was a criminal! Jesus' point in Matthew 5:39-42 is simply that in the kingdom of God, a kingdom that transcends normal social and political boundaries, even this limitation of violence isn't enough. In the kingdom of God, mercy trumps justice. Jesus saw that an invasion was underway—an invasion in which the kingdom of God presses in on the present human world order. In that coming kingdom, love for even enemies was an acceptable manner of life (Matthew 5:44).

Yet even though this movement away from violence is clearly seen in Jesus' use of the older Hebrew Bible tradition, he did not consider that movement in any way a disregard or minimization of that older tradition. Jesus must have been accused of this very thing, for notice just a little earlier in the sermon Jesus clearly expresses his high regard for that older tradition and claims to be fulfilling that older tradition: "Do not think that I have come to abolish the law or the prophets; I have not come to abolish but to fulfill" (Matthew 5:17 NRSV). Jesus is quite able to find grounding for the morality of the kingdom of God in that older Hebrew Bible tradition. Jesus offers a summary statement near the end of the sermon that has become one of the most famous verses in all of the Bible: "So whatever you wish that men would do to you, do so to them; for this is the law and the prophets" (Matthew 7:12). The "law and the prophets" is shorthand for the Hebrew Bible tradition (as it was at that time). Jesus found the precedent for the movement away from violence in the Hebrew Bible itself and extended the trajectory. Jesus simply continued this pulling-forward tradition.

Does the pulling forward of the biblical story create a disconnection between the Old Testament depiction of God and the way the New Testament describes God? Pointedly stated, has the violent God of the Old Testament been replaced by the loving God of the New Testament? Apparently, Jesus didn't think so. In fact, there is plenty of evidence to conclude that Jesus felt quite comfortable identifying with the God portrayed in the Hebrew Bible tradition: "I ask not only on behalf of these, but also on behalf of those who will believe in me through their word, that they may all be one. As you, Father, are in me, and I am in you" (John 17:20-21 NRSV).

Particularly, but not only, in the Gospel of John, Jesus claims that his mission and activity is commissioned by God (John 5:30, 43; 15:15) and is simply a reproduction of God's own activity (John 5:19; 8:38; 12:50). In Jesus' own view, the God of the Old Testament is the God of the New Testament (John 6:38-40; Luke 10:22; Matthew 11:27-28). The evidence provided by Jesus himself suggests that there are connections between the portrait of God in the Old Testament and the portrait of God in the New Testament—connections that we may miss if we read the Old Testament sensitive only to the violence it communicates.

So is the Bible, or parts of it, out-of-date? In some ways yes, and in other ways no. The various parts of the Bible are conditioned by the time and place in which they were written. So yes, the narrow self-interests and points of view that are expressed in, for example, Joshua's command to destroy all the inhabitants of a city or region, cannot simply be applied to all people and at all times. Is the portrait of a nationalistic God of Israel who wars against the national gods of the surrounding nations, which is so common in the books of Joshua and Judges, also out-of-date? Yes, for even in the biblical story line the reader is pulled forward away from that small view of God to a view that sees the God of Israel as the Lord of all, and the same jealous protection and love showered on Israel is freely given to all people. But in other important ways, the early parts of the Bible are not out-of-date at all, for they are regularly pulled forward and given application in new ways. In fact, this way of reading the Bible, by pulling it forward—modeled by Jesus, Matthew, the writer of Hebrews, and others—is a good method for us to try when we read parts of the Bible. The Bible participates in the stream of history that surrounds us all.

VIOLENCE AND THE DIVINE

So, if we agree that there is movement in the biblical story and that not all parts of that story are to serve as models for our own behavior but are pulled forward and given new applications, the question now is: do those early and violent acts and attitudes serve a purpose in the unfolding drama presented in the pages of the Bible? Once again, the answer is yes. This leads us to consider that, in other important ways, the Bible may not be out-of-date at all. Throughout the biblical story God uses violence for a variety of purposes. Biblical writers set forth a number of ideas seeking to explain why bad things happen.

- Suffering is a just result and punishment for sin.
- Suffering is a means to produce a good outcome.
- Suffering is a test of faith.
- Suffering is the result of evil forces warring against God.
- The dilemma of suffering is unsolvable.

It's odd, perhaps, that the Bible offers so many different reasons for violence and suffering. If we are to take the biblical proposals seriously, knowing that the biblical authors offered their respective solutions, often, with full awareness of the other alternatives, we must conclude that the problem of suffering and violence is not a problem like a mathematical equation, requiring only the mustering of the right variables and arranging them in the proper order to arrive at the desired solution. Our question is: do these interpretations have any validity for us as we try to understand the world we live in? Perhaps. There are times when some of the various interpretations the biblical writers offer do apply. Sometimes violence is the result of our own choices. If I choose to regularly wrestle alligators, I should not be surprised if I suffer the occasional nip. It is also true that sometimes violence or suffering can have a beneficial outcome. It's a truism common to all athletes in training: no pain, no gain. But often there is no answer for suffering and violence, and all of the different options granted by the biblical writers seem repugnant.

I remember seeing a photo taken in one of the seaside regions of India shortly after the tsunami of 2004. The picture was of a young boy, no more than five or six, looking directly into the camera—looking directly at me—and weeping uncontrollably as he pulled on the arm of his lifeless mother lying still on the ground. No matter how hard he pulled, his mother would not get up. She could not wipe away his tears. She could not comfort him. It would be damnable to talk to this boy about the benefits of suffering or a punishment for his sin. No, there are times when there is no answer and all we can do is weep.

This conclusion too is present in the pages of the biblical offerings. The writers of Ecclesiastes and the middle part of Job, in particular, find all the conventional answers to the problem of suffering limited and partial in their application. And their response is not to simply conclude: "Aha, I told you! There is no God!" No, for some reason or other, their inability to figure it all out leads them back to God. To be sure, they have no qualms about throwing up their hands in exasperation or uttering the occasional curse born out of frustration, but in the end this problem is simply deposited at the feet of the mysterious and intrusive God—a God who takes pleasure in the work of God's hands. There is no avoidance in their actions, no pretending or wishing the problem would go away, and no blind acceptance. Instead, these writers, who submit the problem of suffering to the mysterious presence of God, agree to live in a tension formed by trust. They have come to accept that "God" is not shorthand for a means of resolving life's problems. They seem to accept that God too is a free agent not bound by mathematical formulae. They also accept that unresolved dilemmas are no more an argument against the existence of God than are the tensions and contradictions in the personalities of our close friends arguments for our friends' nonexistence.

A BIG PICTURE

The Bible is not one book but many, each with its own purpose and plan. At times those books conflict and disagree with one another in perspective or detail. Yet overall there is a general unfolding drama that describes the God of creation actively and intimately involved with what he has made. In this unfolding drama, the biblical writers piece together a grand narrative, attempting to explain the reality of the human condition. The biblical drama opens with the creation of a universe "very good," devoid of violence and the heartache violence leaves in its wake. But, early in the story, the human family made a choice that resulted in devastating consequences not only for us but also for the universe in which we live. Suffering and violence, death and wreckage, were not part of the Creator's design but rather the unintended consequences of humanity's choice to go our own way, to turn our backs on the Creator. Since those early chapters of Genesis, violence has been an uninvited but constant companion of human existence. The Bible is faithful in reflecting this condition. To this point, the story is familiar and uninspiring. What is truly amazing is that there is hope of something different!

The scandal and magnificence is this: in the pages of the Bible, God uses violence and suffering—including his own suffering—for the redemption of humanity from violence and suffering. Throughout the pages of the Bible (Old Testament and New Testament), like a thread binding the whole, God willingly chooses to suffer on behalf of the "works of God's hands" (you and me!) in order to alleviate and eradicate our suffering. The divine heartbreak is expressed powerfully in Hosea:

> When Israel was a child, I loved him,
>   and out of Egypt I called my son.
> The more I called them,
>   the more they went from me;
> they kept sacrificing to the Baals,
>   and burning incense to idols.
>
> Yet it was I who taught Ephraim to walk,
>   I took them up in my arms;
>   but they did not know that I healed them.
> I led them with cords of compassion,
>   with the bands of love,
> and I became to them as one
>   who eases the yoke on their jaws,
>   and I bent down to them and fed them.
> (Hosea 11:1-4)

Here God's anguish is clearly evident. Not only is divine suffering felt because of the child's rejection, but in addition, the pain that the child experiences as a result of the wayward behavior is readily assumed by God! This truly is remarkable. The consistent witness throughout the Hebrew Bible and continued through the Christian New Testament is that God does not remain aloof, an interested but distant observer of our suffering and violence. No. God willingly chooses to suffer with God's creation. It's expressed in a variety of ways. God is "moved to pity" (Judges 2:18); God "hears" their groaning (Exodus 2:24); God is "near" (Psalm 34:18) and present (Psalm 12:5; 73:21-28; 109:31); God is moved to mourning (Amos 2:1-2; Ezekiel 2:10;

Jeremiah 9:10; 12:7; 15:5-9; 31:20); and even gasps in pain: "For a long time I have held my peace, / I have kept still and restrained myself; / now I will cry out like a woman in travail [in childbirth], / I will gasp and pant" (Isaiah 42:14). The crucifixion of Jesus, seen as an expression of divine self-sacrifice, is not a fluke, but is consistent with the self-sacrifice we see from God throughout the Old Testament.

If you take the time to read the whole book of Matthew, you'll find that the descriptions of Jesus take up this theme of suffering. Jesus is presented as willingly suffering violence in order to eradicate violence and make possible a world in which violence has no place—in fulfillment of the Hebrew Bible tradition.

The end of the story is quite remarkable. Whether you choose to end the story at the conclusion of the Old Testament or at the conclusion of the New Testament, there is a hope and a vision of a time when all tears will be wiped away and death and suffering will be no more (Revelation 7:17).

CO-OPTING THE TRAJECTORY—A PREFERENCE FOR VIOLENCE

Unfortunately and tragically, those who claim the Bible as their guide have not always recognized this trajectory to the end of the Bible story. At the beginning of the twenty-first century, one of the chief social functions of religion is to discriminate between people. Religion is used as a marker to determine who is on the inside and who is on the outside. Religion separates people into different groups. We are Muslim or Christian or Jew or Hindu. We label ourselves Baptist or Methodist or Evangelical, Shiite or Sunni. This division is a necessary precursor to religious violence. When relying on biblical precedent, those engaged in religious violence seek to duplicate the early, nationalistic descriptions and ignore completely the pulled-forward quality seen again and again in the Bible.

Violent people have been all too willing to use the Bible for violent ends. I'm not sure any of us could mount a rebuff to the following statement made by Krister Stendahl: "There never has been an evil cause in the world that has not become more evil if it has been possible to argue it on biblical grounds."[3]

So far in this chapter we have considered the violence residing in the Bible and what function that violence may serve in the overarching drama of the Bible. But there is a related problem that we must now think through together. That problem is: has the Bible become co-opted by violent people seeking to make God over into their image?

It is becoming all too plain that the twenty-first century is becoming a century of religious warfare. Religions of all sorts, including Christianity and therefore the Bible, are being swept up in conflicts that threaten to undermine the very structures of religion in general, all in the name of preserving religions in particular. Prejudice, bigotry, fear, and armed conflict have been weapons used to preserve a message of peace. Although rarely seen to the degree that we are now experiencing it, this isn't a new problem. Perhaps the condition is most easily seen in the extreme. David Gushee recently examined the Jewish Holocaust of Nazi Germany, the genocide in Rwanda, and the massacre occurring in Darfur, looking for any sorts of similarities. He concluded:

> The presence of churches in a country guarantees nothing. The self-identification of people with the Christian faith guarantees nothing. All of the clerical garb and regalia, all of the structures of religious accountability, all of the Christian vocabulary and books, all of the schools and seminaries and parish houses and Bible studies, all of the religious titles and educational degrees—they guarantee nothing.[4]

This damning statement expresses concisely a matter that doubters find quite troublesome: to what end? If the Bible can be made to advance violent purposes in such horrible ways, are we better off without it?

These are serious questions with no easy answers. As a teacher of the Bible at a university, I am painfully aware that it is more than likely the terrorists driving the planes bringing down the

World Trade Towers ended their lives while breathing recitations from the Koran. If the Koran could be so misused during an act of violence, why not the Bible? Will someone I teach commit an equally devastating and horrible crime while reciting words from the Bible? Unfortunately, it's no longer unthinkable. And it's a question that resurfaces with growing frequency.

Often the marriage between religion and violence begins with a courtship that appears innocent and, in itself, quite innocuous. I recently attended a baccalaureate service for a local high school. This service provides the religious validation for our community as we send our children off into adulthood. At the conclusion of the service, our children recessed from the ceremony to the strains of "Onward, Christian Soldiers." Our children made their ceremonial transition into adulthood "marching as to war." For many, it was not a metaphor. A relatively high percentage of them will begin adulthood in military uniform. The twenty-first century promises to be a religiously violent epoch in human history. Some of the children marching out of that room will kill people in the name of God and country. I've seen war and know something of the horror it hides. Looking into the faces of our children, I wept.

BETWIXT AND BETWEEN: THE NECESSITY OF DOUBT

You and I find ourselves in a dilemma. We live in a violent world but were made for something else—something else altogether. Our constant challenge is this: to not get used to it; to not get comfortable with violence; to not lose our revulsion and abhorrence, even when we find that violence in the Bible. Patti was right—hell has no place in the world for which we were made, and someday we will be rid of it altogether when, in a strange twist, violence itself will be violently destroyed. Until then, we are betwixt and between—repulsed by the violence we read about in the Bible but anxiously anticipating the end of the story.

In this betwixt and between place, we need more people like Patti. We need more people who will express forcefully and passionately their abhorrence of violence no matter where it's found—even in the Bible. We need more doubters who will call into question the use of the Bible for violent purposes. We need more who are willing to live in the tension betwixt and between. If you find this challenge resonates with you, may I urge you: never forfeit your doubt. The rest of us need you.

CHAPTER SIX

IS THE BIBLE TRUE?

The Bible has some incredible, if not outrageous, things to say. Some of the stories in the Bible seem pretty farfetched. I suspect we could all list our favorites: a boat saving eight people during a worldwide flood (Genesis 6–8); a sea that parts right down the middle (Exodus 14); water gushing out of rocks (Exodus 17; Numbers 20); the sun stood still not once but twice (Exodus 17; Joshua 10); an ax head floating on water (2 Kings 6); and certainly some poor guy getting swallowed by a giant fish only to be vomited up on a beach somewhere (Jonah). This kind of stuff doesn't happen every day. The remarkable isn't limited to the Old Testament. In the New Testament there are stories of people walking on water (Matthew 14:28-29); water transformed into wine (John 2:9); healing those with disabilities (Acts 3:1-10); and of course bringing the dead back to life (Lazarus in John 11:47 and Jesus himself in Matthew 28 as well as the other Gospels). So the question, *Is the Bible true?* seems pretty simple and straightforward. To put it mildly, many of the stories in the Bible require us to stretch the imagination.

Yet despite these amazing tales, when you begin to think about it, the question, *Is the Bible true?* isn't quite so simple as it first appears. It's a difficult question—a question that deserves our attention—in part because there are so many layers to it. First, the question assumes that "the Bible" is a monolithic entity. In reality the Bible is composed of many books, not just one. So the question, *Is the Bible true?* does not take into account for or allow variety among the many voices speaking from the Bible. Second, the question, *Is the Bible true?* suggests that all of the statements in the Bible must be accepted as true before any of the statements in the Bible can be accepted as true. This seems unwise, at best.

For now, it is enough to recognize that the Bible is composed of many books and that these books claim many things. So the question is better phrased, *Are all the books of the Bible accurate in everything they claim?* We will get to the heart of this question in just a bit. First, however, there are some preliminary questions that must be addressed before we consider the matter of the Bible's truthfulness.

PRELIMINARY QUESTIONS: CAN YOU GET THERE FROM HERE?

Earlier, in chapter 2, we discovered that we always come to the Bible by way of some reading conversation. That reading conversation means that if I am to understand the Bible and make some assessment about the truthfulness of what I am reading, I need to understand both partners in this reading conversation: the Bible as it is, and my own circumstance or place in the conversation. We could frame our understanding of the reading conversation in the form of three questions.

1. Is the biblical text before me an accurate presentation of the text the biblical author wrote? Even if we can't do the work of translation or source investigation ourselves, do we have confidence in the work of those who produced the translation of the Bible that is before us?
2. Do I understand the context in which the biblical author wrote? Do I understand how the sentence or truth claim under consideration was understood in

the culture shared by the original author and the original reader or listener?

3. Do I understand the literary form that was being used at the time the text was written? Was the sentence sarcasm, poetry, historical reporting, or something else? Was the sentence or truth claim intentionally inaccurate, exaggerated, poetic, or factual reporting?

We need not and even may not be able to answer all these questions for ourselves, but nevertheless all three of these questions will influence our ability to address the question, *Is the Bible true?* Perhaps an illustration, totally unrelated to the Bible, will help us work our way through the matter without the emotional baggage that often accompanies this question about the Bible.

Let's suppose I give you directions to the local grocery store and in following those directions you become lost or end up at the zoo. It is a fair conclusion that my directions were not true. My statements were not accurate representations of the reality of getting from here to the store. But there are a variety of conditions that may affect the conclusion that my directions were inaccurate. It may be that my statements were simply wrong. My directions did not correspond to the reality of getting to the store. This is a real possibility and should never be dismissed out of hand. However, it may be that my original directions were accurate but the directions were either copied down incorrectly or verbally passed on to you incorrectly by the person to whom I originally gave the directions (question one, above). Or it could be that the context in which the statements were given is different than the context in which the statements were acted upon. It may be that the statements were accurate when they were spoken, but the circumstances may have changed between when I spoke and when you actually went to the store. That is, the store, in the intervening time, may have been torn down or relocated (question two, above). Or, when giving the directions, I might have assumed you were in a car and so used a form of speech appropriate to directions in a car (e.g., go three minutes west and turn right at the first intersection), when, in fact, you were traveling to the store on foot, cutting across yards, vacant lots, and streets. My directions, accurate in the context they were given and using a form of speech appropriate to that context, were inaccurate given the context and forms of speech in which the statements were being received (question three, above). So, as can be seen from this illustration of going to the store, it isn't simply the statement itself that can be true or false but rather that an assessment of the truthfulness of the statement is conditioned by the context in which the statement is placed (either when given or when received). That is, the reading conversation itself may affect the "truthfulness" of the statement I read. When it comes to the Bible, all these possibilities need to be considered in attempting to assess if a statement is true or not.

Only after we have worked our way through the three questions from above are we prepared to address the question, *Is the Bible true?* But, in order to get at the heart of the matter, let's assume that we have worked our way through this series of preliminary questions and have arrived at a satisfactory conclusion to all of them. Let's assume that we have before us an accurate rendition of the text the biblical writer authored. And let's assume we understand the context in which the writer's statements were written. And let's assume we understand perfectly why the author wrote, and the style and form of the writing. With positive answers to all our preliminary questions, we are ready now to get back to where we started: *Is the Bible true?* Or, better, *Are all the books of the Bible accurate in everything they claim?*

Before we go any further, however, two words of caution. First, what follows appears skewed toward finding errors in the Bible. Remember, however, that our goal is to answer the question, *Are all the books of the Bible accurate in everything they claim?* and so we must necessarily focus on the discovery of inaccuracies. This necessary focus of our inquiry will appear unbalanced. Second, the question, *Is the Bible true?* has a history and some baggage attached to it. At the end of the nineteenth century a debate broke out in North America that would influence Christianity for the whole of the twentieth century. Part of the Fundamentalist-

Liberal debate involved disagreement over the character of the Bible. The word *inerrant* became commonly used to describe the Bible as mistake free. The debate, now more than a century old, still influences the way people think about the Bible, and so the question, *Is the Bible true?* is in many circles a hot-button topic that includes a fair amount of emotion. That emotion should not deter us from our inquiry. Rather, it should impress upon us the importance of our quest.

SO LET'S GET ON WITH IT: IS THE BIBLE TRUE?

Typically the question about the Bible's truthfulness is answered in one of two ways. The question is answered as part of a religious presupposition that claims the Bible has no mistakes in it, or the question is answered by looking at all the available evidence—evidence from history, archaeology, and other sciences—to either support or refute the truth claims made in the Bible. Let's consider each of these approaches.

1. IS THE BIBLE TRUE? A RELIGIOUS PRESUPPOSITION

The religious argument for a mistake-free Bible goes something like this: since the original manuscripts of the Bible were in some fashion authored by God, and since God cannot make mistakes, the original manuscripts of the Bible had no mistakes either when interpreted in the fashion intended by that original divine author. The argument goes on to say that whatever mistakes are now present in the Bible have crept in through the years as the Bible has been copied and translated from those originals. The argument hinges on the existence of the original manuscripts of the Bible, and it is precisely at this point that the position fails.

Although there can be no doubt that variations and alterations to the biblical books have occurred—and there is a whole science devoted to identifying these alterations—there are several difficulties with this line of reasoning that leave doubters quite suspicious. First, there are no original manuscripts of any books of the Bible, and so the claim that they are without error cannot be verified. Since there are no "original manuscripts," no one is able to go and check them in order to see if errors have crept in over the years. The nonverifiable nature of the claim leaves many in doubt.

Second, for many of the books in the Bible there never were any original manuscripts, and so the argument is based on a faulty beginning.[1] The whole idea of an original manuscript, as far as the Bible is concerned, is a hypothetical ideal used to provide a standard in comparing various versions of biblical books. The different versions are evaluated according to the standard of that theoretical ideal of the original manuscript in order to identify changes, alterations, and variations resulting in the copying and transmission of those biblical texts over time. The "original" is a theoretical ideal. The fact is that many of the books of the Bible began as oral collections of stories, songs, and proverbs that by their very nature, as oral literature, admitted to considerable variation and disagreement. Even when the books were committed to writing, many of them had various editions in which material was added and sometimes removed.

The prophetic books of the Old Testament provide the easiest example of this last condition. Amos 1:1 reads: "The words of Amos, who was among the shepherds of Tekoa, which he saw concerning Israel in the days of Uzziah king of Judah and in the days of Jeroboam the son of Joash, king of Israel, two years before the earthquake." This introductory verse, identifying Amos and locating him during the reigns of several kings, places the prophetic ministry of Amos "two years before the earthquake." The implication is that this introductory verse, able to reference the earthquake, is separated from the prophetic ministry of Amos by at least two years, since this introductory verse must have been written after the earthquake. Verse 2 adds a second introductory phrase, "And he said," prior to quoting the prophet. The prophet is referred to in the third person and so identified as someone other than the writer of the verse. All this leads us to ask: which was the original—the actual speech performed by the prophet, the quotations of the prophet beginning in verse 2, or the edited book of Amos written by someone other than the prophet and separated by at least two years from the original prophetic speech? The very fact that the book of Amos and most other Old Testament books were edited collections makes the whole idea of an original, at least in the manner thought of today, impossible. An "original manuscript" may be a useful concept in providing an ideal standard while comparing different manuscripts, but as a religious notion the idea is faulty. For most of the biblical books, there never was a pristine original—at least in the sense this religious argument uses for the mistake-free existence of the Bible. If the idea of an original manuscript in which there were no errors is itself faulty, then the foundation is shaken for the religious presupposition of an error-free biblical text.

2. IS THE BIBLE TRUE? LOOKING AT THE EVIDENCE

A second way of answering the question, *Is the Bible true?* utilizes evidence to either support or refute the claim. The evidence can be of two kinds. The evidence can be either (1) in the form of evidence brought from outside the Bible—that is, the way in which the Bible accurately corresponds to and represents the real world around us; or (2) the evidence can be in the form of internal consistency—that is, the way in which all the books of the Bible say the same thing, without contradiction. Let's now consider both types of evidence.

a. Correspondence to the world around us. In attempting to assess the truthfulness of the Bible based on the correspondence of its claims to the world around us, evidence is gathered to show that the biblical claims are accurate in their representation of some external reality—some fact of science or history. That is, did the writer of a biblical book get it right or wrong when reporting on something the writer saw, in describing some geographical fact, or in explaining some event or fact of nature? We will leave aside the whole notion of some grand theory of creation or evolution, for what is allowed as evidence for both is hotly debated. Neither will we consider the reporting of supernatural events, for the supernatural, by its very nature, changes the rules of the game, making external verification impossible. Nor will we consider genealogies, the use of numbers, and many other poetic forms of speech (e.g., circle of the earth, movement of the sun) that are not intended as accurate and factual representations. Finally, we will stay away from occasions where there is reasonable suspicion that the biblical text before us has suffered from alteration in its copying or transmission over time. Instead, we will consider only simple and verifiable observations such as the location of this town or village, or the timing and sequence of some event—claims the biblical writers made that, as nearly as we can tell, they believed were correct. This kind of claim to truth must be verifiable by some condition or source outside the Bible.

Often, the science of archaeology has been enlisted to prove the claims made by the biblical writers. The results have been mixed. Perhaps the best-known example concerns the story of the walls falling down at Jericho. In Joshua 7 a remarkable story is told of a miraculous victory by the invading Israelites under the command of Joshua. Faced with the fortified and well-protected town of Jericho, Joshua instructed the people of Israel in a very unorthodox plan of attack that resulted in the toppling of Jericho's defensive walls. During the twentieth century, archaeologists thoroughly examined Jericho and, sure enough, there are ruins of massive city walls still visible. The problem is these walls were already toppled for a thousand years by the time anybody remotely resembling an Israelite ever ventured nearby! This is an example of a verifiable truth claim that is not supported by evidence from outside the Bible and, in fact, is contradicted by all the available evidence. There are many other examples that could be mentioned, but perhaps it is enough to say here that at many points the Bible's claims and the available historical evidence do not square.

b. Internal consistency. The second way in which the claims of the Bible can be judged true or false is by some sort of internal consistency. If two biblical passages claim to report on the same event and the two passages disagree or contradict each other in some major fashion (more than just on point of view), then it is fair to conclude that at least one of the reporting passages is wrong. If two Bible verses reference the same town, one passage indicating that the town is *east* of city A while the other passage says it is *west* of city A, then logically one of the statements must be wrong (unless the town is, in reality, *south* of city A—then both texts are wrong).

As might be expected, given that the Bible is composed of many books, there are numerous examples of contradiction among the biblical books.[2] Several examples will demonstrate the kinds of contradictions that occur. The Ten Commandments are presented twice in the Old Testament: Exodus 20 and Deuteronomy 5. Both are presented as the very words of God ("and God said"), yet the awkward reality remains: the two don't read the same.

In 1 Chronicles 16:8-36, we are presented with a "song of Asaph" commissioned by David and composed by Asaph, as introduced in verse 7. In reality, the song is a composite drawn from selections of Psalm 105 (vv. 1-15), Psalm 96 (vv. 1-13), and Psalm 106 (vv. 1, 47-48), none of which mention Asaph at all.

In Joshua 10:12-13 a song is presented, spoken by Joshua and addressed to Sun and Moon (v. 12); but in the introduction to the song (v. 12a), it is the Lord who is addressed, not Sun and Moon.

In 2 Samuel 24:1, we are told that the "anger of the LORD was kindled against Israel," and as a result David was incited to conduct a census for which a divine punishment would be the outcome. First Chronicles 21:1 begins to tell the same story as found in 2 Samuel 24 and even quotes from 2 Samuel 24:1, with the exception that it is Satan, not the Lord, who stands behind David's actions.

One set of maps locating ancient Israel among her neighbors is given in Numbers, Deuteronomy, and Joshua, while a quite different set is given in Genesis, Exodus, and the books of Samuel and Kings.

In Mark 11:15-19 the account is given of Jesus disrupting the commerce of the temple by tossing over the tables belonging to the money changers and those selling pigeons for sacrifice. Matthew (21:12-13) and Luke (19:45-48) tell the same story, agreeing with Mark in placing the event just before the time when Jesus would be tried and crucified. John also has an account of the event (2:13-17), but unlike the other Gospels places the event early in Jesus' career, not right at the end.

The events surrounding the resurrection of Jesus; the death of Judas (Matthew 27:5; Acts 1:18); and the use of God's name, Yahweh, (Genesis 13:4; Exodus 6:3) can all be cited as instances of internal contradiction.

Jonah argues against the nationalistic conception of God as portrayed in Hosea and Joel. The Song of Songs celebrates sexuality, whereas Paul favors asceticism. Mark portrays Jesus as a Jewish dissident, whereas Matthew sees Jesus as an observant Jew. Just like the evidence garnered from external sources, the list of instances demonstrating inconsistency between the biblical accounts could also go on and on.

A MIXED BAG

So both types of evidence—external evidence corroborating the Bible's truth claims and evidence of internal consistency between books of the Bible—show that inaccuracies and contradictions do occur within the pages of the Bible. And it does no good to appeal to the accuracy and error-free nature of the original manuscripts because in most cases original manuscripts (especially with the Old Testament) never existed. Yet, to remain balanced, we need to remember that there are many claims in the Bible that are verifiable, that have proved to be accurate, and remarkably so. In some respects, the inaccuracies in the Bible stand out because they are in fact fewer than we might expect.

So in the Bible we are left with a mixed bag. But do *some* inaccurate statements make *all* the statements inaccurate? No, just as some accurate statements do not make all the statements accurate. The biblical books include a mixture. Do these observations regarding external verification or internal consistency make the Bible true or false? No, not necessarily. Point of view, limitations in observation, and inaccuracy in language are all part of reality as we experience it. This was true of the biblical authors no less than for us.

WHAT IS TRUTH?

Do all of the statements in the Bible need to be true before we can accept any of them as true? No. We should expect nothing else. In fact, this mixed bag of claims, some accurate and some not, is itself grounded in the reality you and I experience every day. The Bible is not a fairy tale and as such will not assume fairy-tale-type qualities.

But, if we admit there is the possibility of mistakes, indeed that there are mistakes in observably verifiable assertions, how can we trust that other statements—those we cannot observably verify—are true? Are there other ways to verify the truth claims in the Bible? Yes, I believe there are. Typically we use either logical consistency or physical correspondence as the criterion by which to determine truthfulness (evidence one and two from above). But is there more? Could it be that a measure for determining the truthfulness of the Bible is by assessing the effect it has on those who read it? It may be that the truthfulness of the Bible is best seen, not just in the words on a page, but also in the impact those words have among those who read them.

There is a difference between "true" and the "truth." If you can think back to chapter 2 ("Doesn't the Bible Say Just What You Want It to Say?"), you'll remember that there have been times when the interpretation of the Bible has been dramatically changed by fundamental changes in the way truth was understood. When we see the world around us differently, we tend to understand things like the Bible differently too. We may be at one of those moments in human history again. Think about the following description of the differences between "true" and "truth."

> The distinction isn't just semantic nitpicking. "True" is what we say of a statement we agree with or believe in. "Truth" is a far more nebulous and fundamental concept. We understand it as more of an ideal toward which we strive, rather than one we hold any dominion over. . . . It [truth] is creative, elusive and yet ingrained within the very fabric of our universe. It would exist even if we were not here to discover it or make use of it.[3]

Our answer to the question, *Is the Bible true?* may simply mean that I agree or disagree with the statement made in the Bible. But the question, *Is there truth in the Bible?* gets at something altogether different.

Evaluating the Bible's truthfulness by measuring its effect on people certainly complicates things a bit. But this method of determining the Bible's truthfulness is merited if that impact is the purpose and theme of the Bible. Think of it like this. The truthfulness of a physics book is measured by the accuracy of its physics statements. The same is true with biology, geology, and all science or history books. But the truthfulness of a book of poetry, however, is measured by its ability to touch the emotions and soul of the reader. The same is true for novels, love letters, and blues music. The nature of the biology book's truthfulness is different from the truthfulness of the poetry book. So this begs the question, *What is the nature of the Bible?* At its most basic level, the Bible is about changing the reader. Taken in its totality, the Bible presents to the reader an alternate way of living. This way of life is variously described as a kingdom of God, a new heaven and new earth, or a paradise like the Garden of Eden that reaches beyond the here and now, projecting the inhabitant into a life everlasting. As messy as it may seem, the truthfulness of the Bible is best measured by its ability to transport the reader into that alternate way of living. That some have used the Bible very badly, perverting this alternate way of living for horrible purposes, need not stop us here. Even the persuasiveness of the misuse and perversion points us to something very powerful at work in the Bible.

If this notion of changing the reader is at all close to the purpose and so the measure of truthfulness for the Bible, we do well to consider the kind of change the Bible proposes. Perhaps more important than asking, "Is the Bible true?" is asking, "What is the truth of the Bible?" Permit me to suggest to you that the truthfulness of the Bible is in creating a space to meet God. If this is indeed what the Bible does for the reader, what does that space look like?

A SPACE TO MEET GOD

The Bible came from the same human history we all inhabit. Partial and sometimes-changeable perspectives characterize that history. In the midst of this kind of existence, the Bible creates a space to meet God. Remarkably accurate insights, perceptiveness, factual reporting, as well as internal inconsistency, contradiction, and inaccuracy in reporting external events (some intentional and some not) are all found in the pages of the Bible. Somehow or other all of these form the way the Bible creates this special space in which God is met. So, if all this is really true, what is that meeting with God like?

Given the fact that mistakes, inconsistencies, and contradictions all exist in the Bible, could it be that the process of our own struggle and acceptance, submission and disagreement, accuracy and inaccuracy are all part of the way in which that space to encounter God is formed? By this I do not mean that we accept in the Bible only what we like or what is comfortable to us. No, I mean that we recognize and admit that there are statements in the Bible that for one reason or another we struggle with and cannot accept as true. In this struggle we recognize the integrity of the Bible (it is not simply a mirror we hold in front of ourselves, seeing in the Bible only what we, ourselves, have put there) and we recognize the integrity of our own existence—that our place in time and space does really matter, that our understanding of reality really is important. This struggle is part of the encounter with God. Again, precedent for thinking along these lines is found within the Bible itself. Although their struggles were over slightly different conditions, a struggle between religious belief and experience, the writers of Job and Psalm 73 (vv. 1-3) provide examples of this same kind of conflict.

Here's an example of the struggle drawn from my own experience. I disagree with the way many of the Bible writers disallow women status and respect equal to that of men. There is no getting around it or explaining it away. I understand they wrote from their own patriarchal cultures, and that perspective notwithstanding, I still disagree. Yet could it be that God's word is not in my acceptance of these inequities but in my resistance to these inequities—even if it means "going against the Bible"? Is this what Jesus did in the Sermon on the Mount when he said, "You have heard that it was said . . . but I say to you" (5:21, 28)? Is it possible that disagreements and the recognition of mistakes are important parts of my meeting space with God? Could it be that the movement and expansion of grace, the triumph of forgiveness modeled in the Bible, is a pointer for me to continue down the path in a way that is appropriate to my time and space? Not in a fashion that sets the Bible aside, proclaiming it primitive and irrelevant. No, not at all. "Rather, the Bible requires and insists upon human interpretation that is inescapably subjective, necessarily provisional, and . . . inevitably disputatious."[4] Struggles and disputations are not to be avoided but embraced as part of the space in which we meet God. In our day, gender issues, sexual orientation, and the speed by which changes occur in our understanding of the world around us—including the facts of the Bible, global economic concerns, religious conflict, and health and life concerns—are all contributing to the struggles and disputations encountered when we turn to that biblical space in which we meet God. Could it be that truth—that elusive, creative presence—is in our struggles rather than in the simple biblical assertion alone? Could it be that as we struggle with what is true in the Bible, we encounter truth? If this is at all a possibility, we must now ask, Is it really God whom I encounter in that space the Bible creates? Is the Bible God's word? That last question will guide us in the chapter to follow.

CHAPTER SEVEN

IS THE BIBLE GOD'S WORD?

The phrase *word of God* is often used interchangeably with the word *Bible* as a way of talking about this collection of books. When you stop and think about it, that's quite a claim! In fact, some of the outrageous things included in the Bible (water coming from rocks; seas parting; ax heads floating; and a man, like the famed Dorothy, swirling up to heaven in a fiery tornado) all fade into background noise when compared with this more comprehensive claim—*word of God*. The potential significance of this claim should make any of us stop short and ask, "How do you know?" and "What does it mean?" Not everybody's been convinced. Some have concluded just the opposite about the Bible: "Whenever we read the obscene stories, the voluptuous debaucheries, the cruel and torturous executions, the unrelenting vindictiveness, with which more than half the Bible is filled, it would be more consistent that we called it the word of a demon than the Word of God."[1] *Word of God* or *word of a demon* or something in between—how do we know? A lot of people say a lot of things about this word of God idea, so what does it mean to say that the Bible is the word of God? And why do people believe it?

WORD OF GOD IS AN EVENT, NOT A THING

We need to begin with a very fundamental observation. As a collection of books, the Bible never comes to us unmediated. The Bible is always interpreted. The very fact that the Bible is composed of these individual books and not some others, or that the books are in this order and not some other order, is a matter of imposing an interpretative process on the books of the Bible. Moreover, whether we realize it or not, we all read the words of the Bible out of our own particular set of experiences and way of looking at life. All of us interpret the Bible when we read it. So if the Bible is going to speak to us, it will be in the process of interpretation that it is God's word. Although this may be a self-evident observation, the observation does move us toward an important concept while thinking about the Bible as God's word. God's word is not so much an object—a book on the shelf—as it is an event. The word of God is a communicative event in which God intrudes on us, bringing to us something that is beyond the horizon of our own being or thinking. When we think of the word of God as a communicative event that involves the listener (you and me) as much as the speaker (God?), the quotation up above takes on a different twist. Thomas Paine's rather penetrating statement is as much a statement about himself and his own struggles as it is about the Bible. Whether we agree with him, Paine teaches us that when it comes to hearing the word of God, a healthy dose of doubt is a very good thing.

WORD OF GOD *IN* THE BIBLE

As we begin our quest to understand whether the Bible is the word of God, it is perhaps best to survey what the books of the Bible say on the matter. The results may be a bit surprising. The books of the Bible never make this claim of "God's word" for themselves. At times, some of the books claim to report God's word (whether it is in the form of a vision, a law code, a song, or a dream)[2] and record what they report, but none of the books claim to *be* "God's word." In the Bible, the phrase *word of God* or a similar descriptive phrase (word of the Lord, law of the Lord, and so forth) rarely refers to a written document. The Bible itself does not limit the word of God to a written text or a collection of texts. In the Bible, the "word of God" is a divine communication that occurs in a variety of forms and only gradually begins to coalesce around written texts.[3] For most of the Old Testament biblical writers, the "word of God" or "word of the Lord" is some sort of oral or dreamlike communication and so is a very personal communication between God and a respondent.

For example, Psalm 1 extols the benefits of attention given to the "law of the LORD." Many of us have become accustomed to equating the law of the Lord with the Bible, or at least a part of the Bible. In reality, in Psalm 1 the word translated "law" is better understood as "instruction" or "teaching." The psalm has in mind an application—an intent listening to God's instruction. This instruction, at least as far as this psalm is concerned, is formative for the listener. The instruction changes people.

2 TIMOTHY 3:16

There is a passage from a New Testament book, 2 Timothy 3:16, with something important to say about this word of God idea. Second Timothy 3:16 is a reference often cited to describe the existence and authority of a collection of sacred documents. The verse reads: "All scripture is inspired by God and profitable for teaching, for reproof, for correction, and for training." On the surface of it, the verse seems pretty straightforward. It seems to indicate: given a body of literature that we recognize as God inspired (i.e., God's word), this is how you ought to experience it (teaching, reproof, correction, and so on). But on further examination, the verse is more likely stating something quite different. The verse is better read in this sense: having experienced positive benefits (teaching, reproof, correction, and so on) from documents, what are we to conclude about them? They are God inspired.[4]

This way of reading 2 Timothy 3:16 takes into account several important observations. First, the word translated "scripture" is elsewhere and more frequently translated "writing," in the sense of a book as a writing.[5] When prefaced by a definite article (*the*), the word often means scripture, in the sense of *the* sacred collection of writings (as in 1 Corinthians 15:3 or James 2:8). There is no definite article here, in 2 Timothy 3:16, meaning that a particular or specific set of writings is probably not in the mind of the author of our verse.[6] Second, this suggested way of reading 2 Timothy 3:16 takes into account the fact that when the book of Timothy was written, the Hebrew Bible was still fluid, not firmly established in all three parts,[7] and the documents then being written by and circulating among the Christian communities were exploding in number (more than one hundred that we know of).[8] Scripture, as a sacred canon, was far from set and was more like a three-ring, loose-leaf binder, allowing pages to be added and removed, than it was a bound book with hard covers.

This verse in Timothy is giving to us a very valuable pointer in our efforts to understand the Bible as word of God. The Timothy verse tells us that the word of God doesn't exist as an object that can be put on a shelf or a coffee table for all to see. No, the scripture, as word of God, exists in living interaction with people who are influenced by it. When correction, reproof, and teaching are achieved, somehow or other God is at work and God's word is present. For us, the word-of-God quality of the text is an *event* that occurs, not a thing.

This last observation is important, for it suggests that the Bible comes to us and speaks to us—where we are—in our own context and in our own historical moment. The variations in biblical interpretation that we surveyed earlier (chapter 2) make sense only when we keep in mind that, like the later writers of the biblical text themselves, we too read the text as part of a conversation in which the stable, set message of the original writers speaks to us in our own unique moment in time and space.

WORD OF GOD *FROM* THE BIBLE

Recognizing that others give the Bible the "word of God" label, it becomes worthwhile to unpack the claim a bit and figure out the layers of meaning resident in the claim. Usually people who make the claim that the Bible is the word of God mean that the Bible has some unique truth claim or authority about it. Let's first think together about the exclusive claim to truth resident in the assertion that the Bible is God's word. The truth claim made about the Bible is either that the ideas communicated by the books of the Bible are "God's word" or that the actual sentences—the words, phrases, and unique way they are put together—are uttered by God. If we conclude that it's the words and sentences that are God's word, we are forced to admit that God's word is really only in Hebrew and Greek, with a smattering of Aramaic thrown in (the original languages of the Bible), and, at best, readers of English (or any other modern language) have only an approximation of God's word. This is, in fact, how Islam considers the Koran and why even though most of the Islamic world doesn't speak Arabic, the true Koran is only in Arabic and Arabic remains the language of prayer. For Muslims, God's word is in Arabic.[9]

But most readers of the Bible who claim it to be God's word won't go this far. Very few could read the Bible in Hebrew or Greek, yet that doesn't stop them from making the claim that they know or have experienced God's word. Rather, most who make the claim that the Bible is God's word mean it is the ideas communicated in the Bible that are given this special status. But this poses a problem too. Let's suppose that we are considering a statement found in the Bible, thought to be God's word. That statement is: "Blessed are you poor, for yours is the kingdom of God." This truly is a remarkable statement and you might even recognize it from the Sermon on the Mount as presented in Luke 6:20. The fact of the matter, however, is that I was quoting not from Luke when I wrote that sentence about the poor, but rather from the Gospel of Thomas (54), a book not even in the Bible![10]

Does the fact that I found the sentence in the Gospel of Thomas instead of Luke affect its status as word of God? Or, what do we do with that passage, a little later in Luke 6:42, that talks about removing a log from your own eye before you attempt to clean the speck from someone else's eye? That too is in Thomas (26).[11] If it is the ideas communicated through the Bible that make it God's word, then we must admit that at least some of those ideas can be found elsewhere and that the uniqueness of the Bible as God's word is in question.

The other characteristic meant by the claim that the Bible is God's word is that the Bible is authoritative. I'll admit, we doubters tend to be a bit skeptical here, for all too often the claim that the Bible is the authoritative word of God is invoked only when speakers want to win an argument or promote their own point of view. They can think of no greater authority by which to back up their own correctness and so appeal to the authority of the word of God. But if we return to our earlier observation that God's word is an event, an interaction, the Bible loses some of its value as a tool with which to simply win an argument.

So how is it that the Bible can be God's word? Let's take stock of what we know. The Bible did not fall out of thin air. The Bible is a collection of documents that were (and are) formed by all the twists and turns common to human history. The writers of the Bible did not assume some sort of celestial lectern from which to speak at us or down to us. The books of the Bible were written bottom up—from within the human condition, demonstrating a familiarity with human fears, hopes, desires, and frustrations. The Bible is a book from the inside—from within human history—and it is from within human history that the Bible itself refers to God's word.

When the Bible says that something is God's word, what is usually meant is a moment of deep meaning and influence—a special interaction between a person or group of people and God in which those people are changed, really changed. This is important but rarely talked about. God's word is not the equivalent of a theorem or body of evidence used to prove this or that point. Neither is God's word a trump card used to prove and verify the social authority of a person or group. God's word is an agent of change, uncontrolled and untamed. God's word is a thief in the night, never announced and often unexpected. Yet it is a voice that we can train ourselves to listen for. God's word is an event, not an object on the shelf.

The Bible itself and the majority of Christian thought about the Bible do not equate the Bible and the word of God. In describing the differences between the Bible and the word of God, one writer expressed it like this: "To put it simply, the Bible is not a reference manual. What we seek, rather, is the Word behind the words. . . . We seek not just the plain words of the text, but more importantly the profound witness to which it points. We must be careful not to conflate the two."[12]

DO WE STILL NEED A BIBLE?

Given the past misuses to which the authoritative collection of sacred texts has been put, and the growing likelihood of more misuses in the future, a fair question is, *Is it worth the risk?* Do we still need a Bible? Serious thought by well-meaning people is being given to this very issue. Some have suggested that the books of the Bible invite a dialogue with the reader that is ever changing and that firmly delineating some books as authoritative scripture (canonical) while others are not so esteemed hampers the dialogue.[13] But consider the following:

> It is not the right human thoughts about God which form the content of the Bible, but the right divine thoughts about men. The Bible tells us not how we should talk with God, but what he says to us; not how we find the way to him, but how he has sought and found the way to us; not the right relation in which we must place ourselves to him, but the covenant he has made with all who are Abraham's spiritual children and which he has sealed once and for all in Jesus Christ. It is this which is within the Bible. The word of God is within the Bible.[14]

Consider what would happen if the word of God came only through the spoken word or the performance of a sacred ritual. The human agent, speaking or performing, controls both the spoken word and the ritual performed. But with a book it is different. Simply by being quiet, a speaker can choose who hears. A book has no such choice. Any of us can open the Bible and it must speak. The Bible has always resisted a singular manner of reading and interpretation. For, just like all texts, the Bible cannot choose who reads it, and all readers interact with texts from their own peculiar vantage and point of view. The diversity of readings is reflected in the diversity of communities or groups of people reading. Even if our skills are limited and we struggle over the sentences, we still, in the words of the hapless and illiterate pirate from the *Pirates of the Caribbean: Dead Man's Chest*, "get credit for trying"! That's the wonder of it all: the word of God is found in the words of the Bible and it meets us where we are.

SO WHAT ABOUT ME?

If we take seriously the idea that the word of God is an event, an encounter in which we hear God, the best we can do is talk with one another about what we have experienced. In the following, I have no intention of trying to impose my experience with the word of God on you. Instead, here are some things that have been helpful for me. You may find them useful too.

Years ago I received a great gift for which I will always be grateful. I was given the opportunity to spend a year studying at the Hebrew University on Mount Scopus, Jerusalem. It was a wonderful time for my wife and me. We explored the land together with our (at the time) two young children. The Bible came alive for me in a way it never had before, as together my family and I roamed the hills and ruins—the places I had read about in the pages of the biblical story. Included in my studies were several tutorials that were a real highlight for me. I met weekly with one professor who was both generous with his time and demanding in his expectations. I cherish the memory of those afternoons spent together. As we parted for the last time, this senior professor grasped both my shoulders, looked me straight in the eye, and gave me advice that has burned its way into my thinking. He said: "Since the Bible is bigger than you, be humble. Since the Bible is true, be persistent. And since the Bible is God's word, remember your community responsibility." It's the first of his advice I would ask you to consider in this chapter. The Bible is bigger than any of us, and all attempts to wield power over the Bible are shams and destined to eventual failure. When it comes to the Bible, none of us is complete. We all stand in need of one another. Presumed guides through the Bible who claim otherwise should be avoided. I'm not saying it's a hopeless task and the Bible is forever a closed book. No, not at all! But the largeness of the Bible does make it impossible for any of us to claim final truth about the Bible or its message. The power of the Bible will not be surrendered to those who wish to control it.

How does this influence us, you and me, who simply want to read the Bible? Realize first and foremost, the power of the Bible will never be harnessed or tamed. This makes the Bible, at one and the same time, both exhilarating and frustrating. So my first word of advice is, don't get discouraged—be patient. The Bible is a big book and sometimes hard to read. Don't expect to be able to put it all together, to get it, on the first time through (or second or third). In fact, you may come to find that the Bible is a mine whose treasures are never exhausted. Get ready for a lifelong exploration.

Second, don't be afraid to ask. Other people may indeed have insights to offer. In some ways, I have been very privileged in this respect. I've had the opportunity to listen to and read from the best biblical scholars in the world and often their insights are tremendous. I've also had unexpected, but no less insightful, comments made to me by first-year college students who were opening a Bible for the first time in their lives. These people have, on occasion, literally grabbed me by the shirt collar, about to burst with excitement over something they had read. Help can come from many sources. But as you listen to voices offering help in your reading of the Bible, resist the temptation to elevate those helpful voices to the status of "final word." Nobody has a corner on the Bible. If one of those voices claims some sort of exclusive and exhaustive final word, be careful. You are approaching near an attempt to exercise power over the Bible and, in my opinion, you should think twice.

Third, be willing to be surprised. One of the sure ways to identify someone who has fallen into the trap of attempting to wield power over the Bible is that they have all the answers. They know what the Bible says and can describe its proper application to any and all social questions. The fact of the matter is that in many areas the Bible speaks with many voices and any attempt to make the Bible into a monolithic and single-voiced source of information is a remake and poor shadow of what the Bible really is. More often than not, that one voice originates not from the pages of the Bible but from the mind of the spokesperson who has unwittingly read into the pages of the Bible his or her own bias only to "discover" what they have placed there themselves. We all have this tendency. So how can you and I guard ourselves from this unfortunate, if unintended, attempt to exert our own form of power over the Bible? Be willing to be surprised. This willingness to be surprised carries with it an admission of our inherent limitations when it comes to having a handle on the Bible.

THE BOTTOM LINE

So how do I know that the Bible is God's word? I know because from it I hear God speaking. And how do I know that it is God speaking to me? Because when I listen, the positive changes I experience are beyond my ability to create. If the Bible is the word of God, we, who are intent on listening to God, do well to pay attention to what God speaks about most frequently. Love for God and love for neighbor are far and away the preoccupation of God's voice. The word of God is a redemptive word and the word of God is a creative word. The word of God is calling each of us to a new reality—a reality in which grace, mercy, and forgiveness echo in the ears of those listening to God.

But now a warning, and let me state it bluntly. Any person or group claiming to speak God's word and drawing their identity or reputation from characteristics championing or condemning a particular sexual orientation, the imposition of a prescribed gender role, the maintenance of a certain economic level, or a required militaristic patriotism, has missed the mark. In those instances, the voice of God has been silenced—drowned out by louder and harsher voices. So amid the din of noise, listen carefully. The word of God is known by its fruit, and that fruit is redemption, an offer of hope that someday every part of us will be made right—even those parts we try to protect and hide, those parts we obstinately attempt to keep distant from the overwhelming, uncontrollable, and redemptive love of God.

CHAPTER EIGHT

A SPACE TO MEET GOD?

This book has no answers!
—*Homer Simpson*, The Simpsons Movie

Faced with unpredictable surroundings and desperately seeking help to stave off disaster, Homer Simpson turns to the Bible in search for answers. After quickly scanning through its pages, Homer gives vent to his disappointment and while closing the book with an air of resignation exclaims: "This book has no answers!" Homer isn't alone. When all is said and done, the real question is simply: Does the Bible have any answers? Is there a word from God for me in the Bible?

BY THEIR FRUITS YOU WILL KNOW THEM

If the Bible has answers, it has answers for *someone*. If there is a word from God in the Bible, it is a word from God to *someone*. It does little good to make broad and general claims about the value or importance of the Bible if those claims cannot be tested in the crucible of real life.

There is a story in the Bible that presents Jesus working his way through the matter of finding answers. I think this story is a good starting point for us to begin considering the Bible as a place to meet God. When asked about finding credible answers among the religious authorities in his day, Jesus admits that not everyone claiming religious authority or special knowledge is to be trusted. There are "false prophets," people who either don't know what they're talking about or who are intentionally misleading people, presumably for their own gain. In the midst of this confusing reality, Jesus replies, "You will know them by their fruits" (Matthew 7:16, 20). In other words, put them to the test. If they don't demonstrate a quality of life and morality to be emulated, or if their advice and direction don't have positive results in the lives of others, they are to be avoided—no matter what religious authority they claim or position they hold.

The same test applied to people can be applied to books. You will know the Bible by its fruit. If the Bible is indeed worth our time, it ought to stand the test put to it by Homer Simpson. Does it or does it not have answers? The point is that we can talk about answers from the Bible until we are blue in the face, but it isn't until we actually put it to the test that we will really know if the Bible contains answers for us or if in its pages we too can find a meeting place with God. Previous chapters in this book consider obstacles and barriers preventing a meaningful interaction with the Bible. We have tried to work our way through some of the misuses of the Bible. In this chapter, I'm going to ask you to go ahead and give it a try. See if there's more to the Bible than first meets the eye. See if the Bible is able to produce fruit, beneficial results, for you.

IN THE BIBLE I FIND A SPACE TO MEET GOD

In attempting to be faithful to the test we just established—that the Bible is known by its fruit—the rest of this chapter will be quite personal. I am going to do my best to describe how I've experienced the Bible and how I think I've seen it work for other people. I do not intend that my experience should be a standard that others measure up to—far from it! I intend the following as a conversation between fellow hikers on the trail.

My own interaction with the Bible has convinced me that the Bible has the potential to create a space—a world of its own into which I am frequently drawn. This *space* is different from the one I would otherwise experience, and in this space I am confronted with perspectives that are beyond me. To some degree, this creation of space is a characteristic common to all good literature, art, and theater. The draw of a good book is that it creates a world of mystery or intrigue. When the house lights go down, good theater opens the audience to a new reality. A new world inhabits the stage when the curtains part. In the world of the book or the play, we often encounter ideas, values, possibilities, and ways of looking at things that normally are closed to us. This encounter is the power of the book or the play.

But with the Bible, it's different. It's different because the Person I've encountered is different. In the Bible, a space is created in which I have encountered God. Since, in my experience, God will be neither controlled nor predictable, the encounter is neither controllable nor predictable. Lee McDonald was talking about something very similar when he wrote, "Nevertheless, it must be stressed that the final authority of the church is not the Bible, but the Lord."[1] McDonald's reminder is both timely and unsettling. Things like books and scrolls and written creeds are a whole lot easier to manage and control than are people, especially when the person involved is none other than the Lord of the universe. This space, created by the Bible, is a place in which the reader encounters God, and in that encounter we are not in charge.

When God is met, the Divine's characteristics tend to rub off. In biblical encounters with people, God casts a long shadow over each of them, and the effects of that shadow are not easy to ignore. The world of the Bible, this space in which God is met, doesn't stay there, in the Bible. It has a tendency to leak out, affecting the world of my everyday experience. In this space to meet God the reader is changed, and as the reader is changed, the world of the reader changes also. It's in that change that the Bible works and answers are provided. In my experience, this change has worked out in four interrelated ways.

THE BIBLE PROVIDES A SPACE TO MEET THE UNEXPECTED GOD IN UNEXPECTED WAYS

When read fairly, on its own terms, the Bible provides a space to meet God unfettered by our own preconceptions. We all have ideas of what God ought to be like. This god of our making is, quite often, a composite defined by characteristics or attributes that we find comfortable or at least are accustomed to. Our religious rituals and prayers are full of constraints and pleas, friendly reminders telling God how to act or what we expect from the God of the universe. There is nothing wrong with this. In fact, it's probably a very good thing to develop a habit of expectancy when we approach God. But in the Bible we find more—much more. In the Bible, we enter a space where God is not defined by our expectations and where God acts outside our comfort zone and without our permission. In the Bible, God is no longer bound by our expectations. The Bible gives God free rein and God usually takes it.

Think of it like this. Each one of us approaches God on two levels. On one hand, we approach God through the filter of our own image of what God should be like. In our mental images of God we apply characteristics that either we value or have been taught are appropriate to God. Some of us view God as a compassionate grandfather figure. Others have a mental image of God as angry and vengeful. God is violent—much like a warring Greek deity. Often we have different images for different occasions. The Bible can certainly be used as fodder with which to reinforce our preconceptions of God. We often gravitate to those parts of the Bible that we are comfortable with, parts that fit our expectations, including our expectations of God, while minimizing or ignoring altogether those parts that challenge our preconceptions. This is our "manufactured god." Frequently, this manufactured god is an icon that we hold onto, often desperately, for no other reason than we are accustomed to this god. This manufactured god is, to a large degree, made in our own image to serve our own needs, even if those needs are self-destructive (the need for guilt and disapproval).

But when we do our best to be fair with the Bible, to let it speak in its own voice, one of the amazing things that happens is that we become susceptible to a different sort of interaction with God. At these times, a different God approaches and confronts us: *God the Person*. God the Person is, on the other hand, uncontrollable and certainly not bound by our ideas. The Divine is beyond our expectations and will not be molded into our image. This is the God we meet in the pages of the Bible. The thing is, the God of the Bible will broach no pretenders and it can be painful when God the Person dashes to pieces our manufactured god. Yet it is in this dashing to pieces of our manufactured god that we are prepared to meet the living God. I've found that readers of the Bible go through this process repeatedly. It's a process the writers of the Bible are also familiar with. The wisdom literature of the Old Testament (Job, Proverbs, and Ecclesiastes) calls this meeting and this confrontation the "fear of the LORD." The fear of the Lord is living all of life in the immediate presence of the mysterious and intrusive Creator God—the God of the Bible. This Creator God is mysterious in that this God will never be controlled by our machinations and expectations. God, the Creator, is not our manufactured god, and occasionally the Creator God must break down that manufactured and shadow god. The Creator God is intrusive, never asking permission when reaching into our world and mixing it up a bit. God is not at all averse to introducing complications that upset our status quo, forcing us to confront our own incompleteness. I find that when I read the Bible with a willingness to be surprised, I make myself vulnerable to meeting this intrusive and mysterious God. The Bible can provide a meeting space with God by first of all convincing us that God is bigger and much more complex than what we had thought. In the pages of the Bible, God acts in unexpected ways, preparing us for the possibility of experiencing the Divine in the unexpected.

THE BIBLE PROVIDES A SPACE TO MEET GOD BY OPENING OUR EYES TO A REALITY BIGGER THAN EVER IMAGINED

Psalm 119 is an extended celebration of God's word. Right in the middle of the psalm are two powerful metaphors used to express the benefits available from the word of God (also labeled the law of the Lord, statutes, precepts, testimonies, and so on). The psalmist describes the word of God as a lamp and a light (119:105). This lamp illuminates realities otherwise unseen. It provides a means to see clearly the path stretching before us. Just like a lamp, the Bible illuminates a space in which we meet God, a space in which we can hear the word of God, and a space in which our eyes are opened to a reality larger than otherwise imagined. The writer of Hebrews (perhaps echoing Psalm 33:6) stated it like this: "By faith we understand that the world was created by the word of God, so that what is seen was made out of things which do not appear" (Hebrews 11:3). Like an illuminating beam, the Bible points us to this word of God by which we can see a much larger reality around us. Consider once again the Sermon on the Mount in Matthew 5–7. The sermon begins with a series of "Congratulations!"—the Beatitudes in Matthew 5:3-12. The poor in spirit, the meek, those who mourn, the merciful, and those persecuted are all offered congratulations! If what we see around us is all there is, this series of congratulations is deluded and misguided at best and cruel and hateful at worst. If what we see around us is all there is, this series of congratulations reserves privilege to the few by keeping the downtrodden in their place, telling them it's best if they stay there. But, if there is more, if reality is bigger than what we can see with our eyes, if reality is reflected in that biblical space where we meet God, then this series of congratulatory remarks brings hope to the hopeless and the promise of a future. If this larger reality is in play, then these opening lines of the sermon provide a doorway whereby that larger unseen reality invades the seen reality around us.

The Bible provides answers by making the unseen reality seen. The Bible introduces the reader to a kingdom of God that extends beyond the reality we see with our eyes. But here's the thing, and where, in my experience at least, it isn't always pleasant. This larger reality, this unseen kingdom, provides the possibility of changing the reality that is seen. Because there is more to come, meekness is possible. Because there is more to come, peacemaking makes sense. Because there is more to come, loving your enemy is not a bad idea. The Bible works—the Bible provides answers—by allowing unseen realities to reshape the realities that are seen. The writer of Hebrews calls this having "conviction of things not seen" (Hebrews 11:1). Jesus encouraged us to seek this reality first (Luke 12:31), realizing that it is not coming in observable ways but is already present, right in the midst of us (Luke 17:21-22).

THE BIBLE PROVIDES A SPACE TO MEET GOD BY OFFERING A WAY FOR US TO REDEFINE OURSELVES

One of the real delights in teaching is watching the light come on when a student suddenly understands a theme from the Bible and the personal implications of that theme begin to unfold for that individual. Often a look of puzzlement develops only to be replaced by a distant gaze that descends on the student. He or she stares off into space and then suddenly and furiously begins writing notes that I know have no relation to what I'm presenting in class. These are wonderful moments. Frequently, these "aha moments" involve a deep redefinition by which the person experiencing this moment begins to see himself or herself differently. The Bible provides a forum for a deep self-redefinition. Others have seen this too: "In both Testaments, the divine 'word' is usually experienced as a commanding or commissioning presence that should reorient and renew human lives, individually and communally, in accord with divine priorities."[2] The "divine priorities" that reorient us appear over and over and from cover to cover in the Bible. There are three interrelated and reorienting assertions: *created* by God, *loved* by God, and *forgiven* by God. These are defining categories that have the potential to change any of us in unexpected ways. I admit, I don't think I fully understand the full impact of this redefinition, but in this grand reality made plain in the biblical meeting space with God, this is who we are!

When we allow this redefinition to really grab hold of us and shape the way we think of ourselves, it can result in remarkable changes.

Here's an example of how the way we see ourselves can change the way we live. One of the things I admire about the school at which I work is that the school considers it a valuable part of its mission to give students a chance. Sometimes marginal students are given a chance at a higher education. They are required to work hard and the education is demanding, but they are given a chance. The single most important factor in the success of these students is a change in the way they define themselves. Many of them have ingrained in them that they cannot succeed academically; they define themselves as academic failures. Despite more than adequate ability, their own self-definition prevents their success. If, however, they can begin to see themselves differently—if they can begin to define themselves as academic successes—they begin to live it out and to do well in the university.

The Bible works in much the same way. The Bible offers a new self-definition to those who enter this meeting place with God. Even more dramatically than determining academic success or failure, those who adopt the Bible's vision of self-redefinition—who make it the way they see themselves—are prepared for living in a whole new way: *created by God, loved by God, and forgiven by God.* In the meeting space with God, we discover this is who we really are. And in reshaping our self-perception, this is how the Bible yields its answers.

THE BIBLE HAS PROVIDED A SPACE TO MEET GOD AND HAS CHANGED ME

The Bible has changed me in ways I did not anticipate and, frankly, in ways I did not want. I suspect it will change me yet. Here are some of the ways that several of the biblical writers anticipated the changes produced by entering this meeting space with God.

> And now, Israel, what does the LORD your God require of you, but to fear the LORD your God, to walk in all his ways, to love him, to serve the LORD your God with all your heart and with all your soul, and to keep the commandments and statutes of the LORD, which I command you this day for your good? . . . Be no longer stubborn. . . . Love the sojourner. (Deuteronomy 10:12-19)

> He has showed you, O man, what is good; and what does the LORD require of you but to do justice, and to love kindness, and to walk humbly with your God? (Micah 6:8)

> So whatever you wish that men would do to you, do so to them; for this is the law and the prophets. (Matthew 7:12)

> If you really fulfil the royal law, according to the scripture, "You shall love your neighbor as yourself," you do well. (James 2:8)

Loving the sojourner, doing justice, loving kindness, walking humbly with God, and loving others as yourself—these are transformational characteristics, promising to remake the reader who enters this biblical meeting space with God. These transformational characteristics are remaking me.

NOT FOR THE FAINT OF HEART

All of this means that a serious reading of the Bible is not for the faint of heart. If your experience is anything like mine, you will find that a serious reading of the Bible is quite liable to change you in ways neither of us can predict. I do not know how this meeting space with God works, but I know it does. I've found that in this meeting space I often encounter a sense of quiet and freedom. It is sometimes quite peaceful, involving a sense of God's closeness and acceptance. When I accept God's perception of who I am (*created, loved, forgiven*), a way is paved for changes to occur (Romans 12:2). In this meeting space with God, resources are granted to us that enable a different quality of life (2 Peter 1:3).

But please remember, in this meeting space with God, we aren't in control. You are apt to encounter the unexpected in this meeting space with God. I have found that this meeting space with God is often disturbing, but I've yet to find it distressing. I am often comforted in this meeting space, but I've yet to find it comfortable. So, for now, as you conclude this doubter's guide and as we prepare to go our separate ways, let me encourage you—put it to the test. Put the Bible to the test and see if it has a changing effect on you. But, if after considering the unpredictability of this meeting space with God you find yourself unwilling to take a risk—that you are unwilling to be changed—then let me suggest that the Bible is not for you. You would probably do well in devoting effort elsewhere. However, if you are intrigued by this great and unseen reality made visible in this biblical meeting space with God; if the possibility of a self-redefinition is appealing; if an exploration of what it means to be created, loved, and forgiven by God piques your curiosity, then let me encourage you on.

Put the Guide aside and begin the journey.

APPENDIX 1

SUMMARY STATEMENT OF BIBLICAL BOOKS

OLD TESTAMENT

Genesis: The story of beginnings. The book is divided into two sections. First, the creation of the universe, including the Noah flood story (chaps. 1–12); and second, the story of Israel's forefathers, Abraham, Isaac, Jacob, and Joseph (chaps. 12–50).

Exodus: Tells the story of Israel's miraculous rescue (exodus) from slavery in Egypt. Includes the giving of the Ten Commandments at Mount Sinai.

Leviticus: Composed of two great law codes: the Priestly Code (chaps. 1–16) and the Holiness Code (chaps. 17–26).

Numbers: A compilation of stories during the Israelites' journey from Mount Sinai to the promised land.

Deuteronomy: Moses' farewell presentation before he dies. Includes the Ten Commandments and the "Deuteronomic Code" (chaps. 12–26). Establishes a philosophy of history based on reward and punishment that will guide the narrative of Israel in the books to follow (Joshua–2 Kings).

Joshua: The story of the conquest (chaps. 1–11) and settlement (chaps. 12–23) of the land of Israel under the leadership of Joshua, successor to Moses. The successful occupation of the land is celebrated in chapter 24.

Judges: Accounts of charismatic warlords or "judges" in chapters 3–16. The book ends (chaps. 17–21) with stories designed to prepare the reader for the establishment of the monarchy in Israel.

Ruth: A story, set in the time of the judges, about a Moabite woman who will eventually become an ancestor of David—one of Israel's most famous kings.

1 Samuel: Presents Samuel as the last judge, who will anoint Saul to be the first king over Israel.

2 Samuel: Transitions from the reign of Saul to David to Solomon, the only three kings to reign over the whole nation of Israel.

1 Kings: Presents the reign of Solomon and upon his death the civil war that will divide Israel into two nations: Israel in the north and Judah in the south. Also tells stories about prophets such as Elijah and Elisha and how they functioned as God's spokespersons, warning of a future and sure punishment directed toward a wayward nation.

2 Kings: Stories of the kings of Israel and Judah, ending in the destruction first of Israel by the Assyrians and then the destruction of Judah by the Babylonians.

1 Chronicles: A retelling of the founding of the nation of Israel until the time of David. The story is designed to help those rebuilding Jerusalem, after the exile, connect with the past and develop their sense of social identity.

2 Chronicles: Continues the story of 1 Chronicles, extending the account from Solomon to the beginnings of the rebuilding of

Judah following the exile. First and Second Chronicles uses, at times, Samuel and Kings, but offers many differences in detail and viewpoint.

Ezra: Tells of the rebuilding of Jerusalem under Persian auspices and features the role of Ezra in forming a literary tradition in Israel.

Nehemiah: Set in Jerusalem after the exile, it tells the story of Nehemiah, Persian-appointed governor of Judah.

Esther: The story of Esther, a Jew, who is taken into the harem of a Persian king but through her righteousness is able to save her people from persecution.

Job: An ancient inquiry into the righteousness of God and the matter of hope for humans. Uses a story line about Job, the sinless sufferer, and his friends, who seek to offer him comfort and advice.

Psalms: One hundred fifty (one hundred fifty-one in most Roman Catholic versions) songs and hymns used in worship and prayer, many associated with David.

Proverbs: A collection of wise sayings giving advice so that the reader may be skillful in living.

Ecclesiastes: An inquiry into the meaning of life and the value of both the temporal and the eternal.

Song of Solomon: A collection of love songs celebrating human love, traditionally attributed to Solomon.

Isaiah: Prophecies, oracles, and narratives associated with Isaiah, the Jerusalem prophet living near the end of the eighth century B.C.E. The book contains material much later than Isaiah and, as most of the biblical prophetic books, was edited and expanded over time.

Jeremiah: This is the longest of the prophetic books and is associated with Jeremiah, who lived near the end of the seventh century into the sixth century. Is referred to by New Testament writers as a source for understanding the New Covenant (Jeremiah 31).

Lamentations: A series of laments or mourning songs over Jerusalem. Traditionally attributed to Jeremiah.

Ezekiel: A book of prophecies associated with Ezekiel, a younger contemporary of Jeremiah. Is remarkable for its symbolism and expanding portrait of God, sovereign over all nations.

Daniel: Stories and visions presented as coming from Daniel, a contemporary of Jeremiah, who was taken into exile in Babylon.

Hosea: The first of the Minor Prophets in the Christian Old Testament or the first of the Book of Twelve in the Hebrew Bible. Tells the story of Hosea and his estranged wife, Gomer, as a metaphor of God's relationship with Israel. Set in eighth-century Israel.

Joel: Poems and oracles of destruction, but with a hope toward future restoration.

Amos: A near contemporary of Hosea; also speaks of the destruction of Israel and Judah.

Obadiah: A short prophecy of the punishment coming for Edom because of that people's assistance in Jerusalem's destruction in 586 B.C.E.

Jonah: The well-known story of a prophet swallowed by a great fish only to be spit back out so that the prophet could preach a message of repentance to Nineveh, the great city of the Assyrians.

Micah: Prophecies set in Jerusalem; contemporary with Isaiah.

Nahum: Warnings of the destruction of Nineveh, a great city within the Assyrian Empire.

Habakkuk: Prophecies by a contemporary of Jeremiah about the coming destruction of Jerusalem.

Zephaniah: A harsh critique of social life in Judah prior to the destruction by the Babylonians.

Haggai: A prophetic encouragement to those who return to Jerusalem after the exile.

Zechariah: Contemporary with Haggai; is also concerned with encouraging the work of rebuilding Jerusalem and the Temple.

Malachi: A harsh criticism of social abuses in postexilic Jerusalem.

DEUTERO-CANONICAL BOOKS

(Books found in the Roman Catholic Bible but not in most Protestant Bibles)

Tobit: A story of pious Jews who act heroically with angelic help in the face of political and military persecution.

Judith: The story of Judith and her cunning victory over the commander of the Assyrian army, so saving Israel from certain destruction.

The Wisdom of Solomon: Additional advice for skillful living; attributed to Solomon.

Sirach (Ecclesiasticus): A second-century B.C.E. collection of sage advice.

Baruch: A book attributed to Baruch, Jeremiah's scribe (Jeremiah, chaps. 32, 36), expressing sorrow during the exile and a hope for a future restoration.

Susannah: A short story about a Jewish woman, Susannah, who is falsely accused of adultery by those who attempted to rape her. Daniel figures prominently as the hero of the story.

Bel and the Dragon: Two short stories that contrast the foolishness of idolatry and the majesty of the God of Israel.

Prayer of Azariah: Prayers of three men thrown into the fiery furnace of Daniel 4.

1 Maccabees: An account of the Jewish insurrection against Antiochus Epiphanes in the second century B.C.E.

2 Maccabees: A more legendary and heroic presentation of the Jewish insurrection of the second century B.C.E. and the central role played by the Maccabee family.

1 Esdras: A retelling of parts of Chronicles, Ezra, and Nehemiah.

2 Esdras: A Jewish-Christian work from the first century C.E.

Prayer of Manasseh: A prayer of repentance associated with Manasseh, king of Judah (2 Kings 21; and especially 2 Chronicles 33:13).

NEW TESTAMENT

Matthew: A presentation of the life and teaching of Jesus. An emphasis is placed on characterizing Jesus as the Messiah, the long-expected King.

Mark: The shortest of the Gospels. Many think Mark served as source material for Matthew and Luke. Mark has very little material not shared by these other two Gospels. Together, Mark, Matthew, and Luke are called the Synoptic Gospels because of their similarities.

Luke: Luke is the longest Gospel and may have been intended as volume one of a two-volume set, with Acts serving as volume two. Luke contains many parables not found in the other Gospels.

John: Quite different in presentation from the other Gospels. John is careful to maintain the authority of Jesus and so often appeals to Jesus' self-descriptions.

Acts: Volume two of the Luke-Acts set, Acts traces the growth and spread of the Jesus followers throughout the Mediterranean basin. Prominent in the story is Paul, a missionary, statesman for early Christianity. Acts is a developing self-understanding of the early followers of Jesus.

Romans: Paul's longest letter. The book of Romans develops the theme of "justification by faith."

1 Corinthians: Like many of the Paul letters, 1 Corinthians is a letter Paul sent to a local group of early Jesus followers. The letter answers questions earlier sent to Paul by the believers in Corinth.

2 Corinthians: A second letter answering questions and disputes among the believers at Corinth.

Galatians: Like Romans, Galatians considers the theme of justification by faith, but this time Paul addresses abuses resulting from a misunderstanding and wrongful application of the idea.

Ephesians: A short and general theologically oriented letter, apparently not designed to address any specific concerns. The letter is easily divided into two parts: (1) doctrine, chapters 1–3; (2) application, chapters 4–6.

Philippians: Written by Paul while in prison, Philippians is a joyful encouragement to remain steadfast in faith.

Colossians: Like Ephesians, Colossians is easily divided into two parts: (1) doctrine, chapters 1–2; (2) application, chapters 3–4. This time the doctrinal focus is on understanding the person and work of Jesus.

1 Thessalonians: This letter focuses on the future unfolding plan of God. Perhaps, Paul's earliest preserved letter.

2 Thessalonians: Continues the theme of God's future work.

1 Timothy: Advice to Timothy, a church leader. Together with 2 Timothy and Titus, these three letters are often called the Pastoral Letters. Although written in the name of Paul, these three letters were, most likely, written at a time much after Paul and were written in a manner to imitate this great church statesman.

2 Timothy: More advice to a church leader in caring for other believers.

Titus: Similar to the letters sent to Timothy. The letter deals primarily with interpersonal relationships within the faith community. Titus seems to have lived in Crete.

Philemon: A personal letter Paul wrote to Philemon encouraging him to deal fairly and generously with Onesimus, Philemon's runaway slave.

Hebrews: Sometimes called the "better than" letter, Hebrews presents Jesus as the embodiment of the New Covenant (Jeremiah 31) and so better than the Old Covenant. The letter is an encouragement not to leave the better and fuller life found in Jesus.

James: A sermon presented in the form of a letter that encourages an ethical life.

1 Peter: Like James, many believe 1 Peter to have originally been a sermon. First Peter is designed to offer hope to believers facing persecution.

2 Peter: This brief letter warns against false religious teachers and seeks to focus attention on the return of Jesus.

1 John: This book too may have originally been a sermon and is an encouragement for the faith community to love one another.

2 John: This short book is a warning against false belief.

3 John: This short letter is written to an individual, Gaius. It concerns advice in dealing with a troublemaker, Diotrephes.

Jude: A warning against false teachers.

Revelation: Sometimes called the Apocalypse, the book of Revelation is an example of a popular early form of literature—apocalyptic—that uses symbolism, numerology, and cosmic conflict as a means of communicating messages of hope and confidence in God's final victory over evil and suffering. The book presents the final victory of Christ and a new heaven and earth in which suffering and pain will be no more.

APPENDIX 2

WHICH BIBLE IS THE RIGHT BIBLE FOR ME?

Chapter 2 began by recounting the overwhelming number of different Bibles available on the market today, which are advertised in catalogs and found on the shelves of any bookstore—Christian or not. Amid the great variety, a reasonable question presents itself: which Bible is the right Bible for me? Perhaps now we are ready to answer that question. Unfortunately, the answer is not clear-cut. There is no one right Bible. As we've seen in the brief survey of where the Bible came from, major branches of the Christian church (Roman Catholic, Protestant, and Orthodox) all recognize versions of the Bible that are slightly different in their contents one from another. So the "right" Bible most frequently used in Roman Catholic churches won't be exactly like the Bible used in Protestant churches.

To complicate things even further, there are different English translations of each of these Bibles used by the different branches of Christianity. But take heart! Most of the Bibles advertised in catalogs or standing side by side on the shelf at the bookstore are one of perhaps six to eight main English translations. Most of what differentiates the dozens of different Bibles from one another ("the Bible for . . .") are editorial notes that are designed to help guide the special-interest reader in finding relevant places in the Bible pertinent to that particular interest. So, in finding the "right" Bible, identifying characteristics of these six to eight different translations or versions is most important.

The number of English translations available can be intimidating to first-time readers of the Bible. Below are several considerations to remember when choosing a Bible, followed by a short description of some of the best and most popular English translations.

1. Choose a Bible that was translated by a committee. Page through the introduction or preface of the book and see if the translation committee members are listed. Look for variety among the committee members.
2. Choose a Bible that is formatted in paragraph divisions. First-time readers of the Bible can become easily confused by the way the biblical text is divided into chapters and verses. Some Bibles are formatted with an indentation at every verse, implying that every sentence begins a new paragraph. Choose a Bible with more recognizable paragraph divisions. It will make narrative sections of the Bible easier to follow. Likewise, choose a Bible that has the poetic sections formatted into stanza divisions.
3. Choose a Bible with a modern-language translation. The Bible is hard enough without the additional barrier of *thee* and *thou* and *thou shalt nots*.

Here are some of the better and more common English translations:

New Revised Standard Version: This translation is an update of the Revised Standard Version. The NRSV incorporated more recent linguistic and background information to the biblical text. The NRSV attempts to use gender-neutral language where it's appropriate. The edition published by Oxford University Press contains the Apocrypha and so is suitable for religious use by most branches of Christianity. The NRSV is my recommendation for the first-time Bible reader.

Revised Standard Version: This is has been the standard English translation used in schools and many academic publications since its production in the mid-twentieth century. It is becoming replaced in usage by the NRSV.

New International Version: Produced in the 1970s, this translation has become the most popular English Bible. It is a very readable translation, most popular with conservative branches of Protestantism (it does not include the Apocrypha). The downside of this translation is that the conservative theology of its translators appears to have unduly influenced the translation, at times significantly so.

Revised English Bible: Sponsored by churches from Great Britain and Ireland, the REB is more common in England and Ireland than in North America. The REB is a very readable translation, which includes the Apocrypha, and the edition published by Oxford University Press contains very helpful background notes and articles.

New American Bible: The NAB is the English Bible preferred in Roman Catholic religious settings. Although not to the same degree, the NAB suffers from the same flaw as the NIV, being unduly influenced by a particular theological lens, especially in the explanatory notes and articles.

The Torah—Jewish Publication Society: The JPS is an English translation of the Hebrew Bible and a welcome companion for those reading the Christian Old Testament. The JPS is a very good and readable translation. Remember, the books will be in a different order than that found in Christian Old Testaments and the JPS will have a different feel to it when placed alongside an English Christian Old Testament. I highly recommend it when reading the Old Testament.

King James Version: The KJV was produced in the early seventeenth century and has had a venerable history in the English-speaking world. The beauty of the translation is evident in the poetic sections of the Old Testament (particularly in the book of Psalms). The weakness of the KJV is that it is dated and does not reflect advances in linguistic knowledge of both Hebrew and Greek that have occurred in the past two hundred years. The *New King James Version* is not really a new translation but rather a revision and updating of some of the language in the KJV.

American Standard Revised Version: The ASRV was produced at the beginning of the twentieth century. It sought to incorporate linguistic knowledge unavailable to the translators of the KJV and found a home in many North American Protestant groups because of its improvements over the KJV. Although still used in many church groups, by and large the ASRV has been superseded by the RSV and more recently by the NRSV.

APPENDIX 3

TAKING THE NEXT STEP

The Bible is a difficult book to read. Reliable assistance, providing help in understanding the background, history, and type of writings found in the Bible, can be invaluable to any Bible reader. For those interested in finding more help in understanding the Bible, I recommend the following as a good place to start.

BIBLE INTRODUCTIONS

Bible Introductions provide background help concerning the history of the Bible and offer assistance in how to read the different types of literature in the Bible.

Camery-Hoggatt, Jerry. *Reading the Good Book Well: A Guide to Biblical Interpretation*. Nashville: Abingdon Press, 2007.

Johnson, Marshal. *Making Sense of the Bible*. Grand Rapids: Eerdmans, 2002.

Riches, John. *The Bible: A Very Short Introduction*. Oxford: Oxford University Press, 2000.

BIBLE ATLAS

A good atlas provides historical and geographical information to the reader that often the writers of the biblical books took for granted.

Curtis, Adrian. *Oxford Bible Atlas*. 4th ed. Oxford: Oxford University Press, 2007.

BIBLE DICTIONARIES

Bible dictionaries are similar to encyclopedias, providing numerous articles about all sorts of topics relevant to understanding the Bible.

Achtemeier, Paul, ed. *HarperCollins Bible Dictionary*. New York: HarperOne, 1996.

Sakenfeld, Katherine Doob, gen. ed. *The New Interpreter's Dictionary of the Bible*. Nashville: Abingdon Press, 2006–2009.

REFERENCE BIBLES

A good reference Bible synthesizes the kinds of information found in all of the above types of books and condenses it into one single volume.

Attridge, Harold W., ed. *The HarperCollins Study Bible: Fully Revised and Updated*. New York: HarperOne, 2006.

Coogan, Michael D., et al., eds. *The New Oxford Annotated Bible*. Oxford: Oxford University Press, 2007.

Harrelson, Walter, gen. ed. *The New Interpreter's Study Bible*. Nashville: Abingdon Press, 2003.

NOTES

1. DOES THE BIBLE REALLY MATTER ANYMORE?

1. Adam Bly, "Editor's Letter," *Seed* 2 (March 2007): 6.

2. *CNN Presents: God's Warriors*, "God's Christian Warriors," August 23, 2007.

3. Philip Jenkins, *The Next Christendom: The Coming of Global Christianity* (Oxford: Oxford University Press, 2007), 4.

4. Ibid., 6.

5. Ibid., 7.

6. Ibid., 134.

7. Ibid., 14-15.

8. Ibid., 3.

9. *U.S. Religious Landscape Survey: Religious Affiliation: Diverse and Dynamic* (Washington, DC: The Pew Forum on Religion and Public Life, February 2008) and *U.S. Religious Landscape Survey: Religious Beliefs and Practices: Diverse and Politically Relevant* (Washington, DC: The Pew Forum on Religion and Public Life, June 2008).

10. *U.S. Religious Landscape Survey: Religious Affiliation: Diverse and Dynamic* (Washington, DC: The Pew Forum on Religion and Public Life, February 2008), 5.

11. *U.S. Religious Landscape Survey: Religious Beliefs and Practices: Diverse and Politically Relevant* (Washington, DC: The Pew Forum on Religion and Public Life, June 2008), 3-4.

12. Perhaps best described in *The Gospel of Judas*, ed. Rodolphe Kasser, Marvin Meyer, and Gregor Wurst (Washington, DC: National Geographic, 2006).

13. Alister E. McGrath, *Christianity's Dangerous Idea* (New York: HarperOne, 2007), 462-63.

2. DOESN'T THE BIBLE SAY JUST WHAT YOU WANT?

1. David Mills, *Atheist Universe: The Thinking Person's Answer to Christian Fundamentalism* (Berkeley: Ulysses Press, 2006), 144.

2. Perhaps sensitive to this problem of special interest groups, one publisher has come up with the *CEV Seek Find Bible*, promoted as "the Bible for all people" (New York: American Bible Society, 2006).

3. George Barna provides statistical evidence to suggest that a growing number of committed Christians are experiencing their faith apart from the institutional church. George Barna, *Revolution* (Wheaton, IL: Tyndale, 2005), 29-39.

4. Vincent Miller, *Consuming Religion: Christian Faith and Practice in a Consumer Culture* (New York: Continuum, 2004), 89-93.

5. Julia Corbett, *Religion in America*, 2nd ed. (Englewood Cliffs, NJ: Prentice Hall, 1994), 22.

6. The divisions presented here are adapted from William Yarchin, "Introduction: The History of Biblical Interpretation," in *History of Biblical Interpretation: A Reader*, ed. William Yarchin (Peabody, MA: Hendrickson, 2004), xi-xxx.

7. A very good help in beginning to appreciate the various literary forms in the Bible is Marshal Johnson, *Making Sense of the Bible* (Grand Rapids: Eerdmans, 2002).

3. DOES ANYBODY HAVE THE *REAL* BIBLE?

1. Philip Yancey, *The Bible Jesus Read* (Grand Rapids: Zondervan, 1999), 9.

2. P. J. Tomson, "The New Testament Canon," in *Canonization and Decanonization* ed. A. Van der Kooij and K. Van der Torn (Leiden: E. J. Brill, 1998), 107-31, here 109.

3. The Samaritan community, although not formally recognizable until the third century B.C.E., is a good example of these competing groups and their story of the past, giving a sense of identity to the Israelite community that is quite different from the story presented in Joshua through 2 Kings.

4. Aboth 3:14, *The Mishnah: Translated from the Hebrew with Introduction and Brief Explanatory Notes*, Herbert Danby (Oxford: Oxford University Press, 1985), 452.

5. The writer of 1 Timothy also considers the sayings of Jesus as authoritative "scripture" (1 Timothy 3:18).

6. Geoffrey Mark Hahneman, "The Muratorian Fragment and the Origins of the New Testament Canon," in *The Canon Debate*, ed. Lee Martin McDonald and James Sanders (Peabody, MA: Hendrickson, 2002), 405-15, here 415.

7. An important source of information is found in Eusebius's *Ecclesiastical History* (ca. 325 C.E.), pertinent selections of which are effectively presented by

David Dungan, *Constantine's Bible: Politics and the Making of the New Testament* (Minneapolis: Fortress Press, 2007).

8. Many contend that Marcion was one of the earliest, if not the earliest, to construct a list of authoritative texts for the early followers of Jesus. Certainly, however, all followers of Jesus did not unanimously adopt his list, evidenced by the strong reaction expressed by others (Irenaeus and Tertullian) against the position Marcion held. Lee McDonald and Stanley Porter, *Early Christianity and Its Sacred Literature* (Peabody, MA: Hendrickson, 2000), 612-13.

9. Robert Anderson and Terry Giles, *The Keepers: The Literature of the Samaritans* (Peabody, MA: Hendrickson, 2005), 259-60.

10. Irenaeus provides a good example of an early application of the "scripture" label. "Irenaeus Against Heresies," in *The Ante-Nicene Fathers*, vol. 1, ed. Alexander Roberts and James Donaldson (Grand Rapids: Eerdmans, 1950), 398.

11. One of the most important documents for providing a window onto the early nature of the New Testament is the Muratorian Fragment. Most date the fragmentary document to the end of the second century C.E., although some recently have argued for a fourth-century date (McDonald and Porter, 619). The Muratorian Fragment also includes books that are no longer included in the New Testament: Wisdom of Solomon and Apocalypse of Peter. Lee McDonald, *The Biblical Canon: Its Origin, Transmission, and Authority* (Peabody, MA: Hendrickson, 2007), 369-71.

12. Rowan Greer, "Scriptural Authority (In the Early Church)," in *The Anchor Bible Dictionary*, vol. 5, ed. David Noel Freedman (New York: Doubleday, 1992), 1026-28, here 1027. Lee McDonald extends this list of criteria to five: (1) written by an apostle, (2) orthodoxy, (3) antiquity—written in the apostolic age, (4) inspiration, (5) broad usage. Lee McDonald, *The Formation of the Christian Biblical Canon* (Peabody, MA.: Hendrickson Publishers, 1995), 229-49. Later McDonald suggests six criteria: (1) written by an apostle, (2) orthodoxy, (3) antiquity, (4) widespread use, (5) adaptability, (6) inspiration. Lee McDonald, *The Biblical Canon: Its Origin, Transmission, and Authority* (Peabody, MA: Hendrickson, 2007), 406-20.

13. Ziony Zevit, "The Second-Third Century Canonization of the Hebrew Bible and its Influence on Christian Canonizing," in *Canonization and Decanonization*, ed. A. Van der Kooij and K. Van der Torn (Leiden: E. J. Brill, 1998) 133-60, here 137.

4. IS THE BIBLE SPIN FOR THE POWERFUL?

1. Christian Book Distributors, Christmas Sale Catalog (November/December, 2007), 10.

2. John R. Rice, "Christian Fellowship with Negro and White, Not Intermarriage," *Sword of the Lord* (July 2, 1965): 6.

3. Josh McDowell, *Evidence that Demands a Verdict* (San Bernardino, CA.: Campus Crusade for Christ, 1972); *More Evidence That Demands a Verdict* (San Bernardino, CA.: Campus Crusade for Christ, 1975).

4. You'll remember from chapter 2 that the way people look at the universe around them and the descriptions they use of "truth" vary over time. The way the biblical writers looked at their world is quite different from the way we look at ours.

5. Steven Magill, "Where Will You Spend Eternity?" *Erie Times-News*, Saturday, 22 September 2007, sec. C1.

6. Evident in the famous "battle for the Bible" and seen most clearly in the book of the same name written by Harold Lindsell, *The Battle for the Bible* (Grand Rapids: Zondervan, 1976).

7. One writer expressed it like this: "The authority of the Bible is not found in the words themselves but in the reality to which they point and witness—the Word of God. . . . It is *this* Word that endows the Bible with authority." Frank Matera, "Biblical Authority and the Scandal of the Incarnation," in *Engaging Biblical Authority: Perspectives on the Bible as Scripture*, ed. William Brown (Louisville: Westminster John Knox Press, 2007), 105.

8. Luke 1:3-4 provides another clear example from the Gospels. The Old Testament is the same. Whether it's to promote a specific self-identity in Exodus (12:14, 40), or an ethical behavior in the prophets, or a manner of song and prayer in the Psalms—all have an agenda.

9. See Gerd Theissen, *The Bible and Contemporary Culture*, trans. David Green (Minneapolis: Fortress Press, 2007), xx.

10. Terence Fretheim, "The Authority of the Bible and the Imaging of God," in *Engaging Biblical Authority*, 45-52, here 45.

11. Serene Jones wrote, "When read as an authoritative witness to the real-life truth of God in our midst, the Bible is the place where we are deciphered, translated, figured out, interpreted. . . . It is a book that reveals not just how we see God but, more importantly, how God sees us." "Inhabiting Scripture, Dreaming Bible," in *Engaging Biblical Authority*, 73-80, here 78.

5. WHY IS THE BIBLE SO VIOLENT?

1. Thomas Paine, *The Age of Reason* (New York: Citadel Press, 1991), 182-83.

2. There are in fact two longer epic stories: one modern interpreters call the Deuteronomic History, composed of Joshua, Judges, 1 and 2 Samuel, and 1 and 2 Kings; the second called the Chronicler's History, composed of 1 and 2 Chronicles, and includes (in the opinion of many) Ezra and Nehemiah.

3. Krister Stendahl, "Ancient Scripture in the Modern World," in *Scripture in the Jewish and Christian Traditions: Authority, Interpretation, Relevance*, ed. Frederick Greenspahn (Nashville: Abingdon Press, 1982), 205.

4. David Gushee, "Church Failure: Remembering Rwanda," *Christian Century* 121, no. 8 (April 20, 2004): 28-31, here 28.

6. IS THE BIBLE TRUE?

1. The recognition that no original manuscripts (autographs) exist does not deter the framers of one of the most recent articulations of the belief: "We deny that any essential element of the Christian faith is affected by the absences of the autographs. We further deny that this absence renders the assertion of Biblical inerrancy invalid or irrelevant." Chicago Statement on Biblical Inerrancy: Article X. (www.reformed.org/documents/icbi/html [6-3-08]).

2. Contradiction or lack of internal consistency was much less a problem for those writing the books of the Bible and for the early readers of the Bible because it wasn't until the third century C.E. that the Bible came to be considered one book. With this emerging attitude toward the Bible came also an interpretive drive toward eliminating the differing viewpoints within the Bible. Robert Kraft, "Paramania: Beside, Before, and Beyond Bible Studies," *Journal of Biblical Studies* 126.1 (April 1, 2007): 5-27, here 12.

3. Joshua Roebke, "Truth and Science: A (1842-word) Consideration," *Seed* 2 (March 2007): 61-63, here 61.

4. Walter Brueggemann, *The Book That Breathes New Life: Scriptural Authority and Biblical Theology*, ed. Patrick Miller (Minneapolis: Fortress Press, 2005), 26.

7. IS THE BIBLE GOD'S WORD?

1. Thomas Paine, *The Age of Reason* (New York: Carol Publishing Group, 1991), 60.

2. See 1 Samuel 3:21; 2 Samuel 7:4.

3. J. Sanders, "Word, the," in *The Interpreter's Dictionary of the Bible*, vol. 4, ed. George Buttrick (Nashville: Abingdon Press, 1962), 868-72, here 868.

4. This is in fact very close to the alternative reading supplied by the New Oxford Annotated Bible (RSV) when it reads: "Every scripture inspired by God is also . . ."

5. Persons who write are scribes and what they write is a script and where they write is called a scriptorium (singular) or scriptoria (plural), none of which having any reference to the perceived sacredness of the documents being produced.

6. Unlike verse 15, where a definite article does appear and reference is undoubtedly to some form of the Hebrew Bible tradition.

7. Evidenced just a few verses earlier, where in 2 Timothy 3:8 two people are named as part of the Exodus story (Jannes and Jambres), neither of whom are found in the biblical book of Exodus but come from other ancient sources.

8. An easily accessible comprehensive list is found in the very valuable book by David Dungan, *Constantine's Bible: Politics and the Making of the New Testament* (Minneapolis: Fortress Press, 2007), 148-50.

9. Some, in the Christian community, have come close to this same position in their devotion to the King James Version or some other preferred translation.

10. Elaine Pagels, *Beyond Belief: The Secret of Thomas* (New York: Random House, 2003), 234.

11. Ibid., 231.

12. Michael Joseph Brown, "Hearing the Master's Voice," in *Engaging Biblical Authority*, ed. William Brown (Louisville: Westminster John Knox Press, 2007), 10-17, here 14.

13. Powerfully expressed by Robert Funk, "The Once and Future New Testament," in *The Canon Debate*, ed. Lee Martin McDonald and James Sander (Peabody, MA: Hendrickson, 2002), 541-57.

14. Karl Barth, *The Word of God and the Word of Man*, trans. Douglas Horton (New York: Harper and Brothers, 1957 [1928]), 43.

8. A SPACE TO MEET GOD?

1. Lee McDonald, *The Formation of the Christian Biblical Canon* (Peabody, MA: Hendrickson, 1995), 257.

2. S. Dean McBride Jr., "The Charter of Christian Faith and Practice," in *Engaging Biblical Authority: Perspectives on the Bible as Scripture*, ed. William Brown (Louisville: Westminster John Knox Press, 2007), 112.